**Historical and Cultural Dictionaries of Asia
edited by Basil C. Hedrick**

1. *Saudi Arabia*, by Carroll L. Riley, 1972.
2. *Nepal*, by Basil C. and Anne K. Hedrick. 1972.
3. *The Philippines*, by Ester G. and Joel M. Maring. 1973.
4. *Burma*, by Joel M. and Ester G. Maring. 1973.
5. *Afghanistan*, by M. Jamil Hanifi. 1976.
6. *Thailand*, by Harold Smith. 1976.
7. *Vietnam*, by Danny J. Whitfield. 1976.
8. *India*, by George Kurian. 1976.

Historical and Cultural Dictionary of AFGHANISTAN

by

M. JAMIL HANIFI

Historical and Cultural Dictionaries of Asia, No. 5

The Scarecrow Press, Inc.
Metuchen, N.J.   1976

Printed in the United States of America

Copyright © 1976 by M. Jamil Hanifi

Library of Congress Cataloging in Publication Data

Hanifi, Mohammed Jamil.
  Historical and cultural dictionary of Afghanistan.

  (Historical and cultural dictionaries of Asia ; no. 5)
  Bibliography: p.
  1. Afghanistan--Dictionaries and encyclopedias.
I. Title. II. Series: Historical and cultural
dictionaries of Asia series ; no. 5.
DS351.H36   958.1'003   75-40249
ISBN 0-8108-0892-7

EDITOR'S FOREWORD

The landlocked nation of Afghanistan, situated in Southwest Asia, has historically served as a crossroads for conquerors or empire builders. It is only in recent centuries that Afghanistan has taken a definite territorial form and developed a sense of national identity. Indeed, only in recent months has the nation switched from a long-standing status as a kingdom to that of a republic. This book is particularly timely, not only in its content, but in serving to open the door to more knowledge of this ancient, yet new and intriguing country.

As is the case with all volumes in this series, the authors had the task of rather arbitrarily selecting material for inclusion which is, nonetheless, logical and justifiable. Their assignment also was to be as comprehensive as possible, while maintaining a balanced, helpful, but not necessarily exhaustive, guide and ready reference to the nation. There is no overt attempt on the part of the editor or of the authors to create an encyclopedia although, as it may happen in some cases, any given volume of the series may well be the most comprehensive, contemporary publication pertinent to a given Asian nation which has been published in the Western Hemisphere.

Dr. M. Jamil Hanifi is a Pushtun native of Afghanistan. He received his Ph.D. in anthropology in 1969 from Southern Illinois University and is an Associate professor of anthropology at Northern Illinois University. Professor Hanifi has conducted social anthropological research in Afghanistan and in the United States of America. He is the author of Islam and the Transformation of Culture, and several anthropological articles and reviews in professional journals.

Of particular note in the preparation of this volume has been the collaboration of Mrs. Judith W. Grimes who has regularly served the editor in the preparation of several of the volumes in the series. In this instance, particularly, the amount of basic library search, secondary research and, indeed, some preliminary writing on the manuscript has been of immense value to both the editor and author. To her our sincere appreciation is tendered.

The editor expresses his gratitude to all those persons who helped him in preparing the manuscript for publication.

>Basil C. Hedrick
>Director
>University Museum
>Southern Illinois University
>at Carbondale

INTRODUCTION

Professional and popular interest in Afghanistan is reflected in the large amount of recent research and writing as well as in the increasing pace of socio-cultural dynamics in that country. It is with the hope that this interest will continue to grow and mature that this Historical and Cultural Dictionary of Afghanistan is offered. The proverbial wind of change blowing through Afghanistan has disturbed not only the socio-economic dominance of a few, but the country's entire way of life.

A visitor can observe the effects for himself. He will see a majority of Afghans living in replicas of ancient adobe-like houses and huts; herding livestock and cultivating their farms and plots with home-made implements; pounding and grinding their food in mortars and with primitive watermills; walking for miles in worn shoes and crossing rivers via fragile and unpredictable bridges made of crude rope and wood, and dancing to the music of ancient drums, flutes, and strings. But he will also find most of the "civilized" trappings, many of them far from superficial. He can travel on modern buses and in automobiles and airplanes, and stay in ultra-modern hotels. He can visit urban Afghan houses and be reminded of U.S. cities, especially in the Southwest, equipped with refrigeration and electricity. He will see Afghans working in shops, offices, mines and factories; or growing spices and fruits; herding Qarakul sheep, and making carpets for foreign consumption; leasing or renting land. He will find mosques and schools by the hundreds and more than one university. He can play outdoor games, attend poolside garden parties and performances of amateur dramatics, and buy a flower or a ticket for charity--all of these activities being organized by Afghans. Above all, to an extent not previously dreamed of, this beautiful land is now ruled by progressive and enlightened Afghans, and Afghans themselves are developing new and interesting forms of social organization, cultural and ideological foci.

There are, however, considerable differences in the extent to which particular Afghan ethnic and cultural groups have given up their former habits. Indeed, mostly it occurs that the Afghan individual moving out of the tribal area continues to be influenced by a tribal way of life. Situations vary from group to group within Afghanistan, but in this book I am providing a compendium of <u>selected</u> cultural and historical references to significant spatial and temporal facts about Afghanistan. The book is <u>not</u> intended to be an exhaustive encyclopedic compilation of professional or literary references to Afghanistan. Rather, it is designed so that the categories listed will provide for limited but adequate guidance; fuel to permit further exploration above and beyond what is provided here; and to satisfy and arouse professional, intellectual, humanistic, and personal curiosity. Issue might be taken over the inclusion and/or exclusion of cultural and historical categories in this book. Professional responsibility is accepted by the author for both, but careful attention is drawn to the fact that this is a <u>selection</u> of cultural and historical categories considered <u>significant</u> by a native Afghan cultural anthropologist.

The spelling of proper nouns in Pushtu and Dari is difficult and confusing. No standard, complete guidelines exist, and the reader who might pursue his or her interest in Afghanistan by further reading, study, and research will discover the use of a variety of different systems. For the sake of consistency and easy reading, spellings of native terms are as near as possible to the sounds of the Afghan names, places, events, and things as most of the Afghans pronounce them in their native settings and context.

Dates and statistics are provided when such data have been available. All dates, unless otherwise noted, are in the Gregorian calendar and are exact or nearly exact equivalents of the Afghan solar or lunar calendric dates. Distances, when provided, are generally in approximate miles and feet.

The categories included in the book are organized alphabetically, and cross-references are provided as often as possible to facilitate cohesiveness of the divided text. A selected, comprehensive, and up-to-date bibliography is provided. Note should be taken that the major criteria for selection in the bibliography are substantive value, relevancy, originality, and relative availability.

It is hoped that this book will serve the interests of students, scholars, educators, government officials, businessmen, private and public agencies, and those who are personally interested in the history, society, and ethnic variety of Afghanistan.

The author would like to thank his colleague Donn V. Hart whose "Merry Christmas in May" got him interested in writing this book. Dr. Hart's professional advice and encouragement are greatly appreciated. Another colleague, Cecil H. Brown, provided much encouragement by way of needed reminders to complete this book. I am grateful for this, and promise to reciprocate. Denise D. Mazer and Anita Mozga provided invaluable technical assistance in the typing of the manuscript for this book. Their technical expertise and selfless assistance prevented not so uncommon difficulties and delays. I owe special thanks to Mrs. Judy Grimes who, at the initial stages of the development of this book, provided significant technical and substantive assistance.

The author extends his appreciation for the kindness, understanding, and patience extended by Professor Basil C. Hedrick, the General Editor of the important series of which this book is a part. I wish to express my gratitude to Ms. Vicky Wuehler for her aid in editing of the final manuscript.

To my wife, Marietta, I express my gratitude. Her love, patience, continuous encouragement, and moral support made this possible. Last but not least, I would like to offer my son, Shah Mahmood, an embrace of affection and love for staying out of my way when the going was rough during the research and writing of this book. He is cordially invited to come back in his father's way. His father promises to stay out of his way under appropriate Afghan-Pushtun conditions.

M. J. H.

DeKalb, Illinois

-A-

ABDALI. Known as the Durranis since A. D. 1747 when one of their tribal leaders, Ahmad Khan, was chosen as the supreme chieftain of this tribe. He chose his title to be <u>Durre Durran</u> (Pearl of Pearls) and called himself Ahmad Shah Durrani. Since that time the Abdali have been called Durrani. Two major branches of the Durrani, the Saddozai and Mohammetzai, as royal dynasties, ruled Afghanistan from A. D. 1747-1973. See also AHMAD SHAH DURRANI and DURRANI DYNASTIES.

ABDUL SALAM LOGARI   see   DURAI LOGARI

ABEE. A system of agriculture, prevalent in those parts of Afghanistan where crops are irrigated and irrigation technology is employed. Such a system is found close to rivers or streams where the water needed for irrigation is at once available and predictable.

ABE-ISTADA. A salt lake located about 70 miles southwest of Ghazni, near the town of Muque, in the east-central part of Afghanistan. Its elevation is 7,000 feet and covers an area of about 660 square miles. This salt lake is fed by the waters of the Ghazni River.

ABU-RAYHAN BIRUNI. A poet during the Ghaznavid period who described the "great civilization" in poetic style. He was from Maimandi, what is now Maiwand, near Bost.

ADRESKAN RIVER   see   SEISTAN BASIN

AFGHAN. A citizen, national, or inhabitant of Afghanistan irrespective of language, race, and ethnic affiliation.

AFGHAN DYNASTIES see DURRANI DYNASTIES and GHILZAI DYNASTY

AFGHAN HOUND see GAMES AND SPORTS

AFGHAN INSTITUTE OF TECHNOLOGY. A four-year (post-high school) technical training school built with the assistance of the United States. It has trained Afghans in mechanical, electrical, and civil engineering since the mid-1950s. The Institute is now part of the Kabul University academic and administrative structure.

AFGHANI see CURRENCY

AFGHANISTAN. Situated in the heart of Asia, Afghanistan, "Land of the Afghan," has an area of about 250,000 square miles and a population of approximately 16 million. Afghanistan is a landlocked country, bounded on the north by the Union of Soviet Socialist Republics (Tajik SSR, Turkman SSR, Kirghiz SSR), on the northeast by the People's Republic of China, on the east and south by Pushtun areas of Chitral, Mohmand, Afridi, Waziri, and Baluchistan; and on the west by Iran.
    Afghanistan is the present geographical name of Ancient Aryana. The oldest records of the Aryans, the Vedas (1500 B.C.) and the Avesta of Zoroaster (600 B.C.) refer clearly to the land of the Aryana, around the ranges of the Hindu Kush Mountains, between the Amu Darya (ancient Oxus) and Indus Rivers.
    Afghanistan has been an ancient crossroads and melting pot of different cultures, societies, ethnic groups, and languages. Zoroaster was born in Balkh (Bactria), northern Afghanistan, and there he first preached his religion. Alexander the Great invaded Afghanistan in 332 B.C. and, as was his style, he built "Alexandrias" in many parts of the country. Later, one of his generals founded

the Greco-Bactrian kingdom in the north of Afghanistan, which lasted for two centuries. Buddhism began to penetrate Afghanistan around 250 B.C. and from the 1st century A.D. to the 7th, it flourished in one of its greatest centers in the valley of Bamyan where today the two giant statues of Buddha, the tallest in the world, carved in the face of a cliff, are one of the wonders of the world. From the fusion of Greek and Buddhist art in Afghanistan, the famous and unique "Greco-Buddhist" art was born.

    The Kushans (135 B.C.-241 A.D.), the Sassanians and the Haphtalites or White Huns (241 A.D.-642 A.D.), each in turn, occupied Afghanistan and have left their imprints and vestiges in the history, society, and in the varied cultural plane of this land. Islam entered Afghanistan in the middle of the 7th century A.D., and until today has been the most important principle of social organization and a significant determining factor in the patterning of cultural symbols, value and belief systems found throughout Afghanistan.

AGRICULTURE. About 12 percent of the total area of Afghanistan is cultivated. Over 90 percent of the population is dependent upon agriculture for its livelihood. Based upon Afghan Government statistics the following tabulations provide data for cultivable and cultivated land, major crops, and amount of each crop produced in the years 1969-1970.

Area under cultivation of main crops (in 1,000 hectares--1 hectare = 2.471 acres)	14,000.00
Total area under cultivation	7,844.00
Total irrigated area	5,340.00
Total area under crops	3,420.40
Wheat	2,070.00
Corn	457.00

Ahangar 4

Barley	317.00
Rice	206.00
Cotton	55.10
Sugarbeet	4.00
Sugarcane	2.50
Oilseeds	41.50
Vegetables	91.70
Fruits	136.00
Others	39.00
Total	3,420.40

Production of major crops
(in 1,000 tons) 5,761.00

Wheat	2,450.00
Cotton	785.00
Barley	365.00
Rice	407.00
Sugarbeet	68.00
Sugarcane	60.00
Oilseeds	37.00
Vegetables	671.00
Fruits	842.00
Others	40.00
Total	5,761.00

Yield per hectare
(in 1,000 tons) 60.80

Wheat	1.20
Corn	1.70
Barley	1.20
Rice	2.00
Cotton	1.50
Sugarbeet	14.80
Sugarcane	24.00
Oilseeds	0.90
Vegetables	7.30
Fruits	6.20
Total	60.80

AHANGAR. Ironsmiths. An occupational class usually

found in all cities, towns, and villages in Afghanistan. In towns and villages where there is patterned contact between the settlement and the nomadic group the existence of these specialists is a necessity. The special skills of the ahangar are normally passed from father to the oldest son. Males and females of this class can marry within or without their group.

AHMAD SHAH DURRANI. Sometimes referred to as the first king of Afghanistan. In 1747 A.D. he was chosen the supreme chief of his tribe, the Abdali. Upon becoming the leader of his tribe he assumed the title Durre Durran (Pearl of Pearls) and the Abdali have been called Durrani since then. In a few years he consolidated the warring tribes within Afghanistan and formed one of the largest Muslim Empires in the second half of the 18th century. The Durrani Empire, at its zenith, stretched from Delhi to Western Iran, and from the Amu Darya River to the shores of the Arabian Sea. He was a charismatic leader as well as a distinguished warrior-poet. He died in October, 1772. He is buried in a beautiful tomb in Qandahar.

AIBAK. Capital of Samangan Province. In 1964 the name of the ancient city was changed to Samangan (perhaps to correspond to the name of the province of which it is the capital). The town is about 200 miles north of Kabul. There is an important Buddhist site dating back to the 4th-5th century A.D. The town can be reached by a modern paved road and is known for its embroidered caps (kola). See KOLA.

AI-KHANUM see HISTORY--Greeks

AIMAQ see ETHNIC GROUPS

AIRLINES see ARIANA AFGHAN AIRLINES and BAKHTAR AFGHAN AIRLINES

ALAQADAR. Administrative head of an alaqadari. See ALAQADARI.

ALAQADARI. The smallest administrative, commercial, and communications centers. Some such units have government schools up to the third grade level. These units vary in size with respect to population. The larger the unit in size, the more likelihood of the presence of part-time or full-time specialists such as weavers, artisans, ironsmiths, etc. The larger _alaqadaris_ may be classified as towns while the smaller ones may be categorized as villages. Irrespective of size, the _alaqadari_ population is substantially involved, directly or indirectly, in agriculture and/or horticulture.

ALAUDDIN JAHANSOOZ see HISTORY--Ghaznavid Period

ALEXANDER THE GREAT see HISTORY--Greeks

ALI see KHILAPHATE

ALLAH see ISLAM

ALPTIGIN see HISTORY--Ghaznavid Period

AMIR. A royal title meaning king or paramount chief. Most of the kings of the Mohammedzai Dynasty assumed the title of Amir. See DURRANI DYNASTIES.

AMIR ABDUL RAHMAN KHAN (1844-1901). A charismatic king of the Mohammedzai Dynasty, Amir Abdul Rahman Khan is probably the founder and consolidator of modern Afghanistan as a nation-state. During his reign as Amir (1880-1901) he brought under central control the varied and often opposing tribal units. In doing so, he ushered into Afghanistan for the first time a period of political unity along with some degree of internal stability. The boundaries of modern Afghanistan are, to a large extent, the result of conditional agreements he signed with the governments of Colonial-British India, Iran, and Russia. The eastern and southern boundaries of Afghanistan (the Durrand Line) were unilaterally imposed on the Amir by the British

Colonial Government, and the Amir, more concerned with stability than with boundary demarcation, agreed--but conditionally. The situation was that the Pushtun and Baluch tribes east and south of the Durrand Line would ultimately be incorporated into the boundaries of Afghanistan or would be given a choice to remain independent or be part of British India. This condition has not been honored by the British or by Pakistan which became a state (incorporating the Pushtuns east of the Durrand Line) following the partition of British India into the nations of India and Pakistan.

Amir Abdul Rahman Khan introduced modern administrative and technological principles into Afghanistan from the West with care and discrimination. During his twenty years of government, selected, important foundations for a modernized Afghanistan were initiated. He died in 1901 A.D. and is buried in an elaborate tomb in Kabul.

AMIR AMANULLAH KHAN (1890-1960). Son of Amir Habibullah Khan and grandson of Amir Abdul Rahman Khan, he ruled Afghanistan from 1919 to 1929. He brought with him a new era. Firstly, he declared war on the British Colonials in India. After a military encounter Britain agreed to respect Afghan territory and recognized its complete independence (Britain had previously controlled the foreign affairs of Afghanistan). He was the first Afghan leader to visit several European countries officially and as the head of a sovereign state.

Amir Amanullah Khan introduced revolutionary programs and institutions so as to uplift the socio-cultural lot of Afghan society. During his ten-year rule he initiated reforms in education, social-civil status, science and technology, communications, and in the general area of social and cultural welfare in order to bring Afghanistan into the mainstream of the dynamics of the civilizational processes of his time. The imprints and examples of these reforms are today embodied in monuments and institutions existent in contemporary Afghanistan. Reactionary forces and some elements of the traditional religious groups impeded the pace and full inauguration of these reforms, culminating in 1929 in the take-over of the central government by these elements led by the brigand Bachai Saqqao who for nine months terrorized the Afghan citizenry, fueled the fires of reaction, and temporarily succeeded in stifling the reforms of Amir Amanullah Khan. The Amir chose exile in order to avoid a bloodbath in Afghanistan. King Amanullah Khan died in 1960 in Italy; his remains were brought to Afghanistan and are buried in Jalalabad in a tomb where his father was buried.

AMIR DOST MOHAMMED KHAN. The founder of the Mohammedzai Dynasty, he ruled Afghanistan from 1828 to 1839 and from 1843 to 1863. His first term was interrupted by the first Anglo-Afghan War during which the British Colonialists in India installed Shah Shuja, a member of the Saddozai branch of the Durrani Dynasty, as the ruler of Afghanistan (1839-1842) for his second term. Amir Dost Mohammed Khan regained the throne of Afghanistan in 1843 and ruled for twenty consecutive years. Both his periods of rule were marked by intrigues within and outside Afghanistan for control of the throne. Tribal revolts inside Afghanistan and opposition to the Amir from various tribal-political centers in the country marked the period of his reign. Amir Dost Mohammed Khan died in 1863 in Herat, where he is buried. His sons Amir Sher Ali Khan (1863-1866), Amir Mohammed Afzal Khan (1866-1867), Amir Mohammed Azam Khan (1867-1869), Amir Sher Ali Khan (1868-1879 for his second term); his grandsons, Amir Mohammed Yaqub Khan (1879, son of Amir Sher Ali Khan), Amir Abdul Rahman Khan (1880-1901, son of Amir Mohammed Afzel Khan), his great grandson, Amir Habibullah Khan (1901-1919), and his great, great grandson, Amir Amanullah Khan (1919-1929) ruled Afghanistan without interruption. See DURRANI DYNASTIES. (*Dates in parentheses in this entry refer to the period of rule in Afghanistan.)

AMIR HABIBULLAH KHAN. Son of Amir Abdul Khan, he ruled Afghanistan from 1901 to 1919. According to a treaty signed by him with the British, Afghanistan maintained strict neutrality during the First World War. This, and the usual intrigues common in Afghan kingly dynasties in his family, led to his assassination in 1919 in Jalalabad, where he is buried. His son, King Amanullah Khan, succeeded him to the Afghan throne.

AMIR MOHAMMED YAQUB KHAN see ANGLO-AFGHAN WARS

AMIR SHER ALI KHAN. Son of Amir Dost Mohammed Khan, he ruled Afghanistan twice from Kabul during 1863-1866 and 1868-1879. He is known to have established the first postal mail service in Afghanistan. Amir Sher Ali Khan died in 1879 in Mazare Sharif where he is buried. See also AMIR DOST MOHAMMED KHAN and DURRANI DYNASTIES.

AMU DARYA RIVER (ANCIENT OXUS). This river, which forms the Oxus Basin, rises in the Pamir mountains and flows about 1,500 miles, emptying into the Aral Sea. For some distance it forms the boundary between Afghanistan and the U.S.S.R. The latter uses the river for steamers as far east as Termez, north of Mazare Sharif. Thousands of acres of land are irrigated by the canals into which the water of these rivers is diverted. Important tributaries include the Kokcha, Talegah, and Qunduz Rivers. See also QUNDUZ RIVER, KOKCHA RIVER and RIVERS.

AMULET. An object, often decorative, worn to ward off various difficulties, disease, and potential danger. In addition to protecting against danger, amulets are often also expected to provide strength, wealth, and good fortune. The practice of wearing amulets is common throughout Afghanistan. Usually verses from the Qur'an, written by a Mullah, or an object blessed by a Mullah are wrapped and woven in a piece of cloth or sealed in a small metal container and are worn around the neck, as an armband, around the waist, or around the wrist. Sometimes amulets are woven into the wearer's clothing. A person may wear amulets for both of the above general or specific purposes at the same time. Since children are more prone to disease and misfortune, as well as being the source of hope and aspiration of their parents or elders, they more often and numerically in larger numbers, wear amulets. The Afghan term for amulet is ta'awiz.

ANDKHOI. A town in the province of Fariab, situated in the core of the Turkman area in Afghanistan. It is a center of Qaraqul pelts and the varied and exquisite Turkman rugs--a variation of the famous Afghan carpets.

ANEES. A bilingual (Dari and Pushtu) daily newspaper published in Kabul. One of the oldest newspapers in the country, it was first published as a free paper in 1927. After ceasing publication in 1931, it appeared as a daily under government control and subsidy. After the Republic of Afghanistan was proclaimed in July, 1973, the paper was merged with another government-controlled paper, Islah; together they are subsumed as the Jamhuryat (republic). See also JAMHURYAT and ISLAH.

ANGLO-AFGHAN WARS. The British Government invaded Afghanistan during 1889-1842 and reinstated Shah Shuja on the Kabul throne and deposed Amir Dost Mohammed Khan. The British troops were led by William Macnaghten. The British were brutally defeated in their retreat from Kabul toward India. Macnaghten and Shah Shuja were assassinated in Kabul by Afghan Nationalists and Amir Dost Mohammed Khan assumed the throne once again in 1843. The British occupation and their eventual defeat constitutes the First Anglo-Afghan War.

In 1878, the British, under the pretense of

preventing Russian advances, invaded Afghanistan for the second time. Amir Sher Ali Khan in 1878 had indeed negotiated with the Russians their support of Abdul Rahman Khan (Amir during 1880-1901). While prepared to meet the British threat with assurance that the Russians were not being invited to Afghanistan, Amir Sher Ali Khan died in 1879. His son, Amir Mohammed Yaqub Khan (1879) succeeded him. The British had already advanced into Afghan territory from the east and south. After the Treaty of Gandamak was signed with Amir Mohammed Yaqub Khan on May 20, 1880, the British withdrew from eastern Afghanistan. In the south, however, they were soundly defeated at Maiwand, near Qandahar, by Afghan troops led by the governor of Herat, Mohammed Ayub Khan. Thus, the second Anglo-Afghan War (1878-1880) came to its conclusion. After Amir Mohammed Yaqub Khan's one-year reign, Amir Abdul Rahman Khan, with the understanding that Afghan foreign affairs would be controlled by the British, claimed the throne of Afghanistan in 1880.

The third Anglo-Afghan War (1919) came about when a military confrontation took place near Thal (outside the eastern borders of Afghanistan) in May of 1919 during the rule of King Amanullah Khan. An armistice was arranged. They agreed to recognize the full independence of Afghanistan, including foreign affairs.

ANJUMAN PASS   see   GEOGRAPHY (Central Highlands)

AQ KUPRUK.   A composite of archaeological sites (Aq Kupruk I, II, III, IV) excavated by Louis Dupree. The sites provided a type-sequence beginning with upper paleolithic at lower levels, an Iron Age complex at the middle levels, and material belonging to the Kushano-Buddhic periods is also found. The site is located near the town of Aw Kupruk, south of Mazar-i-Sharif.

AQCHA.   A Turkman town in the province of Jozjan. It is known best for its silver jewelry bazaar.

ARAB. A small ethnic group, primarily located in west and northwest Afghanistan, which claims to be descended from the Muslim-Arabs who introduced Islam into Afghanistan in the 7th century A.D.

ARBAB   see   MALIK

ARCHAEOLOGY. Archaeological research in Afghanistan, however recent, has substantially increased our knowledge of Afghan pre-history and history.
These researches have shed new light on the origin of domestication of plants; the migration and origin of the Neanderthal Man; the Afghan Paleolithic, Neolithic and Chalcolithic (Bronze) Ages; as well as the historic periods establishing definite evidence for the fusion of many cultural traditions in what is now Afghanistan. It has been argued that the evidence for the oldest domesticated wheat exists in Afghanistan. Although most of the archaeological research and excavation has been carried out by American, French, and Italian archaeologists, there exists a young, professionally trained body of Afghan archaeologists whose contributions have already proven important. The Afghan Institute of Archaeology coordinates and encourages archaeological research by professional archaeologists.

ARCHITECTURE. Although in architecture nothing original has been developed since the Timurid period, the traditional techniques of that period have been preserved, including the method of making a faience (glazed pottery with highly colored design) tile.
The use of polychrome faience mosaic to sheet the exterior walls of mosques and tombs is a characteristic of Timurid architecture. The principal elements in the pattern are curving stems, leaves, and blossoms in countless pieces of small, carefully cut and fitted segments of glazed tile.
   The architecture of dwellings is generally of the adobe type. Most houses are cube-like structures with flat roofs. Some of the modern Afghan government buildings are imposing structures designed by foreign and Afghan architects.

Marble is generously used in such structures. In urban areas Western styles of architecture are gradually replacing traditional patterns of the use of space for public and private purposes.

ARDEWAN PASS see PAROPAMISUS MOUNTAINS

ARG. The royal palace built during the reign of Amir Abdul Rahman Khan in Kabul. It housed the Afghan monarchs until the overthrow of the last Afghan king on July 17, 1973.

ARGHANDAB RIVER. An abundant tributary of the Helmand River, it rises in the Southern Hazarajat about 110 miles southwest of Kabul and follows a 350-mile course. About 30 miles after it passes Qandahar it is joined by the Arghastan River and these two join the Helmand River at Qala Bist. See also HELMAND RIVER.

ARGHASTAN RIVER. This river which begins its course about 100 miles east of Qandahar, flows westward for about 170 miles. During its journey it is joined by the Tarnak River 17 miles southwest of Qandahar. Shortly it joins the Arghandab River and at Qala Bist is joined with the Helmand River, ultimately emptying into the Seistan lacustrine depression in the south. See also HELMAND RIVER, SEISTAN BASIN and TARNAK RIVER.

ARIANA AFGHAN AIRLINES. The international airline of Afghanistan. It has air service to New Delhi, Amritsar (India); Tehran (Iran); Beirut (Lebanon); Peshawar, Lahore (Pakistan); London (England); Istanbul (Turkey); Tashkent, Moscow (U.S.S.R.); and Frankfurt (West Germany). Other international airlines flying to and from Afghanistan are: Aeroflot, Pakistan International Airways, Iranair, Indian Airlines, and Lufthansa.

ART AND HANDICRAFTS. No great sculptor or painter has emerged since the 16th century in Afghanistan. Only calligraphy and illumination have been encouraged and preserved, but professional practice has become almost extinct with the introduction of the printed book. An Arts College was established in Kabul in the 1930's. It holds an annual exposition, the "Autumn Salon." Most of the works are oil paintings or water colors of scenes, gardens or mountains, or depictions of major events in Afghan history. A style of miniature paintings is maintained and carried out in Herat using techniques described in ancient manuscripts. Other painters, especially during the 1960's are noted for their use of strong colors.

Theater arts are very new in the country. There are only four theaters, two in Kabul, one in Herat and one in Qandahar. Traveling companies take plays to provincial cities and appear sometimes at local fairs. Secular plays, in Dari or Pushtu, are either original adaptations of European classics or Arabic or Turkish comedies. Some of the original plays have moral themes, such as wasting time, while others are designed to appeal to the comic sense of the audience.

Handicraft work forms an important segment of the economy, and some handicraft products, especially carpets are world famous. Leather works and pottery are produced almost universally. Istalif, a small resort town, about 15 miles north of Kabul, is noted for a particularly fine, blue glazed pottery. Metal workers produce trays, pots, ewers, and basins which are found in most city, town, or village bazaars. Metalworkers of Badakhshan and Qandahar pattern intricate designs in copper utensils, and those of Ghazni and Kabul use bronze to make such household goods. Knives are made all over Afghanistan, but the knifemakers of Charikar are the best known.

Nuristan is important for woodcarving. The Nuristanis not only make furniture and cooking utensils, such as dishes and milk pails of wood decorated with incised patterns, but also carve the doors and windows of their houses as well as their gravemarkers.

The most important handicrafts are the

weaving of cotton, woolen and silk cloth, feltmaking and carpet weaving. Using simple looms, cotton weaving is done in nearly every town and village of the north and northeast provinces. Felt for use in making tents, blankets, floor coverings and clothing is made in the Hazarajat and the northern provinces. Some are used in natural colors; others are dyed or decorated with intricate designs.

Of the handicrafts, only carpets are exported to a significant extent. Excellent in quality, they are famous throughout the world for their brilliant colors. The art of carpetmaking is highly traditional, and the majority of patterns are guarded family secrets handed down from generation to generation over the centuries.

ARYAN   see   HISTORY--Indo-Aryans

ARYANA   see   HISTORY--Indo-Aryans

ASADABAD. Capital of Kunar Province. It is located about 55 miles northeast of Jalalabad. It is one of the two large towns in Afghanistan with Nuristani population. Situated at the confluence of the Panjsher and Kunar Rivers, it attracts tourists during national holidays, especially Jeshn (the Independence Celebration) which is colorfully and enthusiastically celebrated. The construction of a new highway and the building of a small modern hotel will make Asadabad easily accessible and attractive. A lumber mill located near the town is designated to capitalize on the forest resources of Kunar Province.

ASHOKA. Emperor from about 273-232 B.C., he was the grandson of Chandra Gupta Maurya. After some great military victories, resulting in 100,000 deaths to the enemy, he was overtaken by guilt and remorse and spent the rest of his ruling years spreading Buddhism throughout the empire. He eventually became a Buddhist monk and attempted to spread this religion even to foreign lands.

Stones, columns, and rocks were inscribed with his admonitions, and one which is in both

Greek and Aramaic, has recently been discovered near Qandahar. It calls for a cease in hostilities bringing harm to other people and even calls on hunters and fishermen to abstain from their sinful activities. He calls upon his people to listen to and obey their parents and elders, particularly men. See also HISTORY--ACHAEMENIDS.

ASMAR FOREST. Located in the southeast foothills of the Hindu Kush, this forest is the center of much of Afghanistan's forestry production. Lumber is transported on the Alishang and Alinghar Rivers to the Kabul River.

ASYAB (Called Zranda in Pushtu). A watermill found in Afghan agricultural villages. Every large village, or a number of small closely situated villages will have an Asyab. An Asyab is usually owned by the largest landowner in the village and the farmers pay for its service either in grain or in cash.

ATABI. A prosaic style chronicler who lived during the Ghaznavid period.

ATAN. Also called "Atan-i-Milee," it is the national dance of Afghanistan. During celebrations such as weddings and other festive occasions men and women form a circle clapping and going around (usually to the right) with alternating footsteps to the gradually increasing pace of the rhythm provided by drum, and wind and string instruments. The dance is originally Pushtun in character and was diffused to other areas of Afghanistan over the past forty to fifty years, when many Pushtuns were encouraged to settle in other areas of Afghanistan. Among Pushtuns, men and women perform the dance separately, the Pushtu epic verses are sung along with the music. In other regions, particularly in urban areas, men and women perform Atan together.

AVESTA. The definitive compendium of scriptures and

precepts of Zoroastrianism was probably written
during the reign of Cyrus the Great (599-530 B.C.).
Some historians believe that the earliest references
to what is presently Afghanistan are found in the
Avesta. See also HISTORY--Indo-Aryans.

AVICENNA see IBN-SINA

AZAN. From the Arabic A'Dzan, the Muslim call to
prayer made by a mua'zin from the minaret of a
mosque. The believers are called during specific
times of day to pray alone or collectively. See
also ISLAM and FIVE PILLARS OF ISLAM.

-B-

BABUR see ZAHIRUDDIN MOHAMMED BABUR

BACHAI SAQQAO. The son of a Tajik water carrier, he
occupied Kabul in January 1929 and ruled for nine
months. The progressive reforms set in motion by
King Amanullah Khan were dealt a reactionary blow
by Bachai Saqqao. Nine months after his takeover
he was captured and put to death by King Mohammed
Nadir Shah. In some Tajik folklore, Bachai Saqqao
is called Habibullah Ghazi.

BACON, ELIZABETH (deceased, 1972). A pioneer
American ethnologist who did systematic social
anthropological research among the Hazaras of
Afghanistan and other cultural groupings in Central
Asia. Her contributions to the Culture Area classification of Asia are still the primary references
for students of ethnology interested in Asia, particularly Afghanistan. Her publications on the
Hazara are classic examples in methodology,
theory, and thorough ethnography in social anthropology.

BACTRIA. The archaeologic ruins of a Greek settlement
are found here, dating to 300 B.C., when Alexander led an expedition to Central Asia and Northwest

India. It turned out to be only a raid, but this settlement, between the Oxus and the Hindu Kush, was left. Greek colonists and their descendants remained for two centuries and ruins include large halls lined with stone columns with carved forge capitals and stone sarcophagi statues. Much of this may have been destroyed around the 2nd century B.C. by Asian nomadic invaders.

BADAKHSHAN (PROVINCE). A northeastern province of Afghanistan which ranks fifth in size among the twenty-seven provinces of Afghanistan. The province is famous for the towering icy peaks of the Pamirs in its eastern fringes as well for the excellent horses it provided to the caravans of the 13th century. The economy of the province is based primarily on agriculture, though mining is also an important industry. Virtually all the lapiz lazuli mined in Afghanistan comes from Badakhshan Province. Silver, copper, and lead mines and deposits also exist in Badakhshan. The scenic beauty and variety in Badakhshan is probably best described by Marco-Polo who traveled through this area about 600 years ago: "Between the mountains are the wide plains clothed with grass and trees, and large streams of the purest water spurting through clefts in rocks. In these streams are trout and many other fine sorts of fish."

BADAL. The Pushtun term for blood revenge. The society is organized on many principles of reciprocity. In the event a Pushtun group is beset in a manner which compromises its fundamental values (e.g., regarding the sanctity of life, marriage, prestige, honor, the chastity of its female members, and other core values), then reciprocal action, preferably the killing of the guilty party or a member of his group, will be incumbent upon the group which has suffered such infliction.

BADGHIS (PROVINCE). A province in the northwest part of Afghanistan. Badghis is the tenth largest province in area in Afghanistan. It ranks 24th in

population in the country among the 28 provinces.
Major crops are pistachio nuts and wheat. Since 1964, however, efforts have been made to diversify the economy. Experimental farms have been working on new kinds of sheep and improved varieties of cereal grains. An experimental institute has been established to teach more people the skill of making mawri carpets. These carpets are very well known and have long been a product of Badghis. To increase production of these famed carpets an institute has been established to teach the skill to more people.

BAGHLAN. Capital of Baghlan Province. It is located about 165 miles north of Kabul. It is presently the center of health projects, agricultural experimental projects, and increasing industrial complexes. Cotton, wheat, sugarbeets, fruits, and sheep breeding are the principal experiments being carried out in the area. A sugar factory is located in the city. Sculptures dating to the Kushan period have been found in Baghlan.

BAGHLAN (PROVINCE). Located just north of the Salang Pass, this province is a booming agricultural and industrial area. It is a major center for health projects, agricultural experimentation, highway construction, and industrial expansion. A malaria eradication campaign has been very successful in this area. Pilot projects aim at setting up a community health service center for each 10,000 people.
New highways (the Salang highway and the Doshi-Shairkhan Bandar highway) have placed Baghlan in closer proximity to other industrial, commercial, and administrative centers of Afghanistan.
Wheat and rice are the traditional crops.
Industrial plants in the province are located in the cities of Baghlan and Pule Khumri. Two dams have been built on the Ghori River to produce power for local industry--including a cement factory and a textile plant in Pule Khumri.

BAGRAM see KANISHKA THE GREAT

BAIHAQI. A prosaic style chronicler who lived during the Ghaznavid period.

BAKHTAR AFGHAN AIRLINES. The domestic airline of Afghanistan with regular air service to provincial capital cities and some other remote areas within Afghanistan.

BAKTASH   see   RABIA BALKHI

BALA HISSAR. "High Fort." Most historical cities in Afghanistan have a Bala Hissar. The Bala Hissar of Kabul has been the scene of many fateful events for Afghanistan, and is no doubt the most important (and the largest) of the Bala Hissars found throughout Afghanistan. It is situated in the southeastern part of Kabul City, and if a visitor's permit is available, provides a most panoramic view of the valley of Kabul. The Bala Hissar was used as a palatial military fort until 1880. It is no longer used for such purposes. For students of Anglo-Afghan Wars and the internal political dynamics during the 19th century, the Bala Hissar of Kabul provides the central stage for the evolution of socio-political processes in Afghanistan.

BALKH   see   BACTRIA

BALKH (PROVINCE). A province located in north-central Afghanistan whose capital is Mazare Sharif. It ranks 18th among the provinces of Afghanistan in area. Balkh served as the chief commercial area of the Amu Darya plain commanding the trade routes to the south over the Hindu Kush to India, in the north to Transomiana, and to the east to China for most of its 5,000 years. Today, Mazare Sharif, the capital city, has grown to be the industrial and cultural center of Balkh and is also the major city in the fertile plain of the Balkh River. This city houses a new textile plant which is to produce ten to fifteen million meters of cloth annually. Cotton is a major crop in the province. Raisins are an important crop, as are melons and qaraqul. Attempts are being made to increase the amount of water available to farmers. There are many skilled craftsmen in the province who make very fine rugs and weave silk known as alacha. The old pottery-making tradition is being revived. See also MAZARE SHARIF.

BALKH RIVER. An important water source for the agricultural area in the north. It also supplies water for the irrigation system extending around Mazare Sharif. It rises 40 miles southwest of Mazare Sharif at the confluence of two small rivers, its waters coming from the western foothills of the Hindu Kush.

BALUCH see ETHNIC GROUPS

BAM-I-DUNYA. The "Roof of the World" or the high country located in the Wakhan Corridor.

BAMYAN (CITY). Capital of Bamyan Province situated about 200 miles northwest of Kabul. It is a small town lying at the heart of the Hindu Kush in a valley containing the colossal Buddhas of Bamyan. The tallest Buddha, 175 feet tall, dates back to the second half of the 3rd century A.D., and the smaller Buddha, 125 feet, was built during the 5th century A.D. There are also wall paintings and stucco decorations dating from late 5th to early 7th centuries. The statues and the artistic manifestations of Bamyan indicate a mixture of Indian, Central Asian, Iranian, and classical European art styles and motifs. There are other Buddhic and Islamic sites in and around the Valley of Bamyan. The town is accessible by road and air service.

BAMYAN (PROVINCE). This province, located in central Afghanistan, has an area of 20,242 sq. km. -- ranking 14th among the 24 provinces in size. Its capital is Bamyan. This area--once a center for Buddhist pilgrims--was destroyed by Genghis Khan in the 13th century and remained isolated in the Hindu Kush peaks. Travel by land has been difficult because of the many narrow valleys lying between the Hindu Kush and Kohe Baba peaks (often reaching 5,300 meters). A new highway and airport, however, are making access to the valleys easier for both tourists and residents. The iron mine on the border with Wardak Province is also more accessible and is important to the economy. Wheat and barley and some cattle, sheep and horses are raised. Parts of two statues of Buddha are still found in the Valley of Bamyan. They were originally built between the 2nd and 4th centuries under the patronage of the Kushans. The smaller one was about 120 feet high and the larger, 175 feet high. They were defaced, however, when Genghis Khan conquered the valley in revenge after his grandson was killed there. Besides the Bamyan Valley, tourists are also attracted to the Band-i-Amir lakes (q.v.) which are three hours by road from the valley. Other valleys in the province which are noted for their beauty are the Karghanalou, Shahidan, Shibartoo, and Surkhdara.

BAND-I-AMIR LAKE(S). A group of five lakes located west of Bamyan. They feed the Bamyan stream. Natural dams separate the lakes. The blue lakes have a very beautiful shape and hue, and are filled with large trout.

BAND-I-TURKESTAN MOUNTAINS. A range along the northern edge of the Murghab River Valley, which is about 100 miles long. It lies north of the Paropamisus Mountains. The lower northern hills of this rugged chain are used as a breeding ground for the Qaraqul sheep (q.v.). The highest peak is the Zangilak, 11,590 feet high, located about 45 miles southwest of Maimana.

BARTH, FREDRIK. A well known European social anthropologist who has done extensive social anthropological research among Pushtuns and Baluchs. His works are pioneering efforts both in ethnography and social anthropological theory. See also Bibliography.

BAYAN RANGE see GHOR (PROVINCE)

BAZAAR. The major shopping area and/or the central market place in Afghan cities, towns and villages.

BEHZAD. A famous artist of the Timurid period (late 15th century). He was the leader of the school of manuscript illumination which developed a miniature style combining great technical skill with studied naturalism. Behzad exercised great influence on his contemporaries and upon successive generations of painters.

BENAWA, ABDUL R. An important contemporary Pushtun poet. He is mostly known for his landay style of poetry which usually entails a first line of nine syllables and a second line of thirteen syllables. He is the author of several major poetic works in Pushtu.

BIST see BOST

BOGHRA CANAL see HELMAND VALLEY

BOKHARA see HISTORY--Islamic Period

BOST. Capital of the province of Helmand. Remains of a royal castle and military camp probably dating back to Ghaznavid times when Bost was the second capital of the empire after Ghazni have been found here. When Zaranj was destroyed during the Arab invasions, Bost became a major city and remained a cultural capital until it was destroyed by Sultan Aluaddin Jahansooz, looted by Genghis Khan, and ultimately ruined by Tamurlane (see TIMURE LUNG) when he demolished the dikes in the 14th century. Later, during the time of Amir Habibullah, the construction of the Nahre Seraj Canal to irrigate lands east of the Helmand was an attempt to rebuild the area. Bost is located about 90 miles west of Qandahar. See also HISTORY--Ghaznavid Period.

BRAHUI see ETHNIC GROUPS

BUDDHA see GAUTAMA BUDDHA

BUDDHISM see HISTORY--Buddhist Period, HINAYANA and MAHAYANA BUDDHISM

BURQA see CHADARI

BUZKASHI see GAMES AND SPORTS

-C-

CALENDAR. Calendars printed in Afghanistan delineate three systems: Shamsi (solar); Qamari (lunar); Gregorian. The Shamsi calendar resembles the Gregorian in that the months always occur in sequence at the same time of the year. Afghanistan adopted a Shamsi calendar during the reign of King Amanullah Khan. Qamari months occur eleven days earlier each year, rotating around the seasons, completing a full cycle every 32.5 to 33 years. Both the Shamsi and Qamari calendars date from the Hijra, the migration of the Prophet Mohammed and his followers from Mecca to Medina. Therefore the year 1 in the Muslim dating system equates with 622 A.D. The following tables illustrate the different systems:*

Shamsi Months in Dari	in Pushtu	Number of days	Astrological Symbols	Gregorian equivalent of 1st day of month
Hamal	Wray	(31)	Aries (Ram)	March 21
Sawr	Ghway	(31)	Taurus (Bull)	April 21
Jawza	Ghbargolay	(31)	Gemini (Twins)	May 22
Saratan	Chungash	(31)	Cancer (Crab)	June 22
Asad	Zmaray	(31)	Leo (Lion)	July 23
Sunbullah	Wazhay	(31)	Virgo (Virgin)	August 23
Mizan	Telah	(30)	Libra (Scales)	September 23
Aqrab	Lärum	(30)	Scorpio (Scorpion)	October 23
Qaus	Lindah	(30)	Sagittarius (Archer)	November 22
Jadi	Murghoma	(30)	Capricorn (Goat)	December 22
Dalwa	Salwagah	(30)	Aquarius (Water Carrier)	January 21
Hoot**	Kab	(29)	Pisces (Fish)	February 20

*The equivalencies are for 1968-69 A.D.
**Hoot has 30 days in leap year

CAPISA see KANISHKA THE GREAT

CAROE, OLAF. A renowned orientalist who has written extensively about the Pushtuns of Afghanistan. He is the author of a major work (see Bibliography) about the Pushtuns as well as an authority on the ethnohistory of other Central Asian socio-cultural groupings.

CHADAR. A scarf worn by both the peasant and urban villagers to cover facial areas. It is a symbol of modesty and indicator of adulthood among Afghan women.

CHADARI. A long, head-to-toe garment designed to cover the female completely. It is worn in addition to and over regular clothing. It is worn when women go outside the family compound to shop or to visit close relatives. It is most common among urban (city and town) populations. It resembles a tent-like garment whereby only the area covering the eyes is made of gauze-like material so the women can see out. The Chadari comes in different qualities of cloth and many different colors. Only the quality of the cloth may serve as an indicator of socio-economic class. However, often enough the lower socio-economic strata of the urban population use expensive cloth to make them indistinguishable from upper class groups. The Chadari was outlawed in 1959 under the Premiership of Mohammed Daud (now the President of the Republic of Afghanistan) as a step towards further emancipation of women in Afghanistan. In spite of this, it is still worn by urban and town women throughout the country, but its use is on the decline.

CHAGHCHARAN. Capital of Ghor Province. It is located west of Kabul and east of Jam, the site of the famous minaret of Jam. The town is situated on the banks of the Hari Rud River and is accessible by gravel road. This city was chosen as the new capital in 1964 owing to its central location.

CHAIKHANA. A teahouse (literally, Chai=tea; Khana=house). Found in most every village and town, the Chaikhana is the center for discussion, refreshment, and rest. These teahouses are found in all parts of Afghanistan. Most Chaikhanas also serve food--eggs and nan (the unleavened Afghan bread) for breakfast; Shorwa or soup for lunch; and Palaw (rice and stewed meat) for dinner. In larger towns one may find large Chaikhanas called Hotel or Rustoorant. The quality of food in the Chaikhanas varies from one ethnic area to the other. In towns situated on major highways one can expect a Chaikhana open around the clock.

CHALCOLITHIC. The copper age. Some important chalcolithic sites dating from the fourth to the first millennia B.C. have been excavated in Afghanistan. The chalcolithic pattern discovered in Afghanistan is one where a semisendentary situation is predominant. The period was marked by the seasonal migration of animals to pasturelands, with the bulk of the population remaining in farming villages.

CHAPAN. Overcoat or homemade cloak used by villagers, city and townsmen in the cold season. It is generally a quilted garment of many colors made in northern Afghanistan, and now exported to other Afghan areas. The quilted variety is worn in cold weather, while a lighter version is used during warm seasons.

CHAPANDAZ. A horseman who plays buzkashi. The province of Fariab is the home of most of the best buzkashi horsemen. See also GAMES AND SPORTS.

CHAPARIS. A structure, built by farmers in the province of Ghor, which is erected in the fields during the summer months and used as a temporary home. It consists of a wooden framework covered with bamboo matting, is domed and often has elaborate decorations like those of the miniatures.

CHARIKAR. Capital of the province of Parwan in east-

central Afghanistan. It is known for its knives--
pocket-size to daggers. They are made of scrap
metal and have handles of wood, pearl, horn, or
bone. This city, located about 40 miles north of
Kabul, is a popular picnicking place from March
to April.

CHENGIS KHAN (Also spelled Genghis Khan, Jenghis
Khan). A Mongol chieftain during the 13th century
who penetrated deep into Afghanistan, killing countless men, women, and children, destroying homes,
flocks, crops, and so on. While traveling south
from the city Bamyan in the Valley of Bamyan, the
son of Chengis Khan, Mutufer, was killed in battle.
Out of revenge for this, Chenghis Khan leveled the
city and slaughtered the populace. A descendant
of his, Tamerlane (A.D. 1336), followed a very
similar pattern. A grandson of Chengis Khan was
Kublai Khan.

CHIHL ZEENA. "Forty steps." A rock-cut chamber
high above the plain at the end of the chain of
mountains forming the western defenses of the old
city of Qandahar. It is located about three miles
west of Qandahar on the road to Herat. Forty
steps lead to a chamber (which might have been
used as a throne at ceremonial occasions) which is
guarded by two lions. The chamber is partially
defaced and is inscribed with an account of Moghul
conquests.

CLIMATE. Information about the climate of Afghanistan
is based on the rainfall and temperature recordings
of the meteorological stations established since
1946. In general, Afghanistan has a semi-arid
steppe climate with cold winters and dry summers.
A sub-arctic climate with dry and cold winters
dominates the mountain regions of the northeast.
In the mountains cutting across the eastern Pushtun
areas a divergent fringe effect of the Indian monsoon, coming usually from the southeast, brings
maritime tropical air masses which dominate the
climate in the area between July and September.

At times, these air masses advance into Central
and Southern Afghanistan, bringing increased humidity and some rain.

Dust whirlwinds ("dust-devils") frequently
occur during the summer months in the plains of
the southern southwestern parts of the country.
Rising at midday or early in the afternoon, they
advance at velocities ranging between 50 and 100
miles per hour, raising towering clouds of dust.

Temperatures and precipitation are controlled by the exchange of air masses. The highest
temperatures (over 95°F.) and the lowest precipitation (less than six inches annually) prevail in the
drought-ridden southwestern plateau, stretching
over the western and eastern boundaries of Afghanistan.

The central highlands, with its highest peak
ascending toward the Pamir Knot, represents
another distinct climatic region. From the Kohe
Baba Range to the Pamir Knot, January temperatures may drop to -5°F. or lower in the highest
mountain areas, whereas July temperatures vary
between 50° and 80°F., depending on the altitude.
In the mountains the annual mean precipitation,
much of which is snowfall, increases eastward and
is highest in the Kohe Baba Range, the Western
part of the Pamir Knot, and the eastern Hindu Kush.

Precipitation in these regions and the southeastern monsoon area is about 16 inches a year.
The Wakhan corridor, however, with temperatures
ranging between 50°F. in the summer to below
-5°F. in the winter, receives less than four inches
of rainfall annually. Permanent snow covers the
highest mountain peaks. In the mountain regions in
the north-northeastern part of the country, the snow
is often seven to eight feet deep during the winter
months. Valleys become snow traps, as the high
winds sweep much of the snow from mountain peaks
and ridges.

The climate of the Northern Plains of Afghanistan represents a transition between mountain and
steppe climates. Aridity increases and temperatures
rise with descending altitudes, becoming highest

along the lower Amu Darya and in the western parts of the Plains, in the provinces of Fariab, Badghis, and Herat.

CLOTHING. Most Afghans dress similarly from the neck down according to sex. In both cases, however, the basic dress consists of loosely tailored shirts (for women it often reaches the ankles) and bloomers. Ethnic differences are expressed in headgear for both men and women. Men wear turbans and turban caps. The style of the cap and the manner in which a turban is tied reflects ethnic identity; the quality of the cap and turban as well as the size of the turban reflect economic status. In urban areas the Western style of dress and clothing, both for men and for women, is increasingly used. See also CHADARI and CHAPAN.

COAT OF ARMS   see STATE EMBLEM

COCKFIGHTING   see   GAMES AND SPORTS

COMMUNICATIONS. Telephone service with and between large Afghan towns and cities as well as with most of the countries of the world is available. Modern telegraph service for national and international use is publicly available. The national postal service of Afghanistan is adequate and effective. See also RADIO AFGHANISTAN, ARIANA AFGHAN AIRLINES, and BAKHTAR AFGHAN AIRLINES.

CONSTITUTION. The constitution of 1964 was suspended after the Afghan Republic was declared. Work continues on the formation of a new, democratic, and republican constitution.

CROSS-COUSIN MARRIAGE. Marriage between the children of brother and sister. Cross-cousin marriage is widely practiced throughout Afghanistan, with preference given to the pattern whereby a man marries his mother's brother's daughter. However, the most preferred pattern of marriage is parallel-cousin marriage. See also PARALLEL-COUSIN MARRIAGE.

CURRENCY. The _afghani_ is the basic unit of currency. It is divided into 100 _puls_. Coins are issued to the value of 1/4, 1/2, 1, 2, and 5 _afghanis_, and notes to the value of 2, 5, 10, 20, 50, 100, 500, and 1000 _afghanis_.

CYRUS THE GREAT see HISTORY--Achaemenids

-D-

DAILY PRAYERS. One of the five major tenets of Islam. All Muslims are required to pray five times a day: early morning, noon, early afternoon, late afternoon, and evening. These prayers can be performed individually or collectively in a mosque or elsewhere. The Friday noon prayer is performed collectively in a community mosque. Since one of the reasons for these prayers is to express social solidarity, it is preferred but not required, that these prayers be performed collectively. Only adults are required to perform the prayers. When praying collectively, women and men pray separately. When praying, a person must be ritually cleansed through the process of ablution. If one can maintain the state of cleanliness, no other ablution prior to praying is necessary if one has been performed earlier. However, the early morning prayer must be preceded by a ritual cleansing process. See also FIVE PILLARS OF ISLAM.

DAIWA DAILY, THE (THE LAMP). The newspaper of Sheberghan, capital of the province of Jozjan. The two-story building which houses the newspaper also has a library which may be used by the general public.

DAQIQI see HISTORY--Islamic Period

DAR UL AMAN. About six miles from the center of Kabul, Dar ul Aman was designed as a new capital city of Afghanistan by King Amanullah Khan. As one approaches Dar ul Aman an impressive castle (of European architecture) is noticeable along with its gardens and surrounding parks. This building was designed for the parliament and the national secretariat. The building, however, was never used for its original purpose. Another large palace, in European style, is located nearby.

DARE ZANG. A Valley in the province of Fariab where many residents and tourists go during the hot summer months. Lovely waterfalls are found here, as well as hot springs. One of these springs is known as a wishing spring. When a person visiting the spring makes a wish, a stream of fresh water spurts out from the spring if the wish is to come true.

DARI see LANGUAGES

DARIUS I (522-485 B.C.) see HISTORY--Achaemenids

DARUNTA DAM. Located in the Nangarhar province, this dam generates power for domestic and industrial use and also makes possible the irrigation of 30,450 hectares of land. It is one of the major agricultural and hydroelectric projects in the country.

DASHTE MARGO. A vast plain of mixed sand, loam, clay, and gravel located in the southwest part of the country. It lies between 1,500 and 2,000 feet above sea level, covering an area about 170 miles long and 90 miles wide. It is bordered by the Khash River on the north and the Helmand River on the east and south.

DASTAR (MANDEEL, or LUNGI). The turban which is wound around a small cotton skullcap. See also CLOTHING.

DEH. A common term referring to a village and particularly to compound names indicating specific villages: first, those which occur along rivers and permanent streams, and second, those which cluster around a town, or several such clusters surrounding a city. The second type of village is more common in Afghanistan.

DEH MORASAI GHUNDAI. An archaeological site, excavated by Louis Dupree in 1951. It dates to the Bronze Age. It is located just outside Qandahar. See also MUNDIGAK.

DEHQAN. The Afghan reference to a farmer or a peasant. The occupation of farming or peasantry is called Dehqani. About 90 percent of the Afghan population are Dehqans.

DISEASES. In the absence of reliable statistics regarding disease, health statistics are based on secondhand information, speculation, and the random reports of foreign personnel. In the late 1960's the main causes of debility and death were gastrointestinal infections, tuberculosis, communicable diseases of childhood, venereal diseases, trachoma, and malaria. Nutritional deficiency diseases, often due to lack of protein, as well as anemia, were frequently underlying causes of debility. Vaccination campaigns have reduced the incidence of formerly dreaded epidemics of smallpox and cholera.

DIWAN   see   KHWAJA ABDULLAH ANSARI

DODAI   see   NAN

DUPREE, LOUIS. A prominent contemporary American anthropologist who has spent more than twenty years in ethnological and archaeological research in Afghanistan beginning in the early 1950's. He is probably the most published anthropologist on Afghanistan. Dupree, in addition to his own research and writing, has helped the institutionalization of anthropological study and research in Afghanistan. He has, in addition, stimulated, helped, and directed the professional study and research interests of scores of Afghan and non-Afghan scholars. His writing on the ethnology of Afghanistan is extensive and is the standard reference for scholars interested in the anthropology of Afghanistan. See also Bibliography.

DUPREE, NANCY. A contemporary American author who has spent many years of residence in Afghanistan. She has written extensively on Afghanistan. Of particular value are her published historical guides to Afghanistan and to the various important cities and major points of interest in the country. Nancy Dupree has been of much help to the Afghan Tourist Organization in the agency's efforts to stimulate tourism throughout Afghanistan. See also Bibliography.

DURA BAZI. Whip racing. A game played with two teams. One team member goes over to the other team's side and is chased back by an opposing team member who tries to whip him. When they have crossed the field, roles are reversed. Though there is no declared winner, the ones who are whipped the least are the most admired.

DURAI LOGARI. A musician from the province of Logar who has helped to make the distinctive songs and sounds of the music of his home region familiar (via radio) to people in all parts of the country. His son, Abdul Salam Logari, often accompanies him.

DURRANI DYNASTIES.

The Saddozais

Ahmad Shah	1747-1773
Timur Shah	1773-1793
Shah Zaman	1793-1799
Shah Mahmood	1799-1803
Shah Shuja	1803-1809
Shah Mahmood (return)	1809-1819
Civil War	1819-1826

Durrani Tribes   34

The Mohammedzais

Amir Dost Mohammed Khan	1826-1839
Shah Shuja (Saddozai-return)	1839-1842
Amir Dost Mohammed Khan (return)	1843-1863
Amir Sher Ali Khan	1863-1866
Amir Mohammed Afzal Khan	1866-1867
Amir Mohammed Azam Khan	1867-1868
Amir Sher Ali Khan (return)	1868-1879
Amir Mohammed Yaqub Khan	1879-1879
Amir Abdul Rahman Khan	1880-1901
Amir Habibullah Khan	1901-1919
Amir Amanullah Khan	1919-1929
Revolution and Bachae Saqau (not a Mohammedzai)	1929-1929
Mohammed Nadir Shah	1929-1933
Mohammed Zahir Shah	1933-1973

DURRANI TRIBES. These tribes are located in the west and southwestern parts of Afghanistan. The major Durrani tribes include nurzai, achakzai, alizai, popalzai, barakzai, mohammedzai, and alikozai.

-E-

ECONOMY. The economy of Afghanistan depends primarily on the traditional occupations of stockraising and farming, which engage about 90 percent of the population. Agriculture, including animal husbandry, furnishes more than 75 per cent of the country's exports. Aside from providing raw materials for a rudimentary industry, agriculture also supplies most of the basic food needs with the exception of wheat, sugar, and tea. Ranking after agriculture and stockraising, trade and services contribute the next largest share to the national income. Since most internal trade involves exchanges between villagers and nomads, such as wheat for livestock and livestock products, commercial trade consists largely of exports and imports of manufactured items and those consumer goods which the family (the basic self-sufficient socio-economic unit) cannot produce itself. Bazaars serve both as wholesale and retail exchange points. The paving of most of the roads around Afghanistan which connect the major cities increasingly facilitates the transport of goods from production to consumption centers.

Afghanistan is heavily dependent on importation of capital goods, processed industrial raw materials, and most manufactured consumer goods.

Handicraft industries continue to be more important than factory industries. In terms of the available resources, industrial potential considerably exceeds the ability to mobilize capital for development. Consumer goods industries predominate; modern plants are few, largely producing textiles and cement. Many smaller enterprises produce flour, sugar, vegetable oils, procelain, footwear, glassware, and leather. Together with numerous handicraft industries, they supply most of the country's household consumer requirements, hand-woven carpets being the major export item. Factory industries have not yet produced a surplus for export, but they serve to decrease Afghanistan's dependence of certain imports.

EDUCATION. Education is provided free to all Afghans through state-supported schools. In addition, education through the third grade is mandatory (when accessible). Over the last fifteen years educational facilities on primary, secondary, and senior high school levels, as well as on the university level, have been expanded and are on the increase. See also QAYYUM, NAWABZADA ABDUL.

ELECTRIC CURRENT. Voltages of 200-220 A.C. and cycles of 50/60 are common throughout Afghanistan.

ELPHINSTONE, MOUNTSTUART. A 19th century British ethnographer. His ethnographic writings on Afghanistan are the oldest of their type. His one major definitive work (see bibliography) is an important ethnographic sourcebook on Afghanistan.

ENTRY POINTS. Visitors traveling by automobile or bus can enter Afghanistan from the west through Islam Qala, west of Herat; through Torkham, east of Jalalabad; and through Spin Buldak, southeast of Qandahar. All international flights must land at Kabul or Qandahar International Airports.

EPHTHALITES see HISTORY--Buddhist Period

ETHNIC GROUPS. Afghanistan is a mosaic of ethnic, socio-cultural, and linguistic variety. The following can be considered as the major ethnic groups in Afghanistan:
Aimaq: There are about 800,000 aimaqs in Afghanistan. They speak a dialect of Dari with a significant amount of Turkic vocabulary. They are situated in the northwest part of Afghanistan and belong to the sunni sect of Islam.
Baluch: About 100,000 live in Afghanistan, leading a nomadic or semi-nomadic life. They live primarily in the southwestern part of Afghanistan. Some of the Baluch have been relocated in northern and northwestern Afghanistan. They speak Baluchi and belong to the sunni sect of Islam.
Brahui: A major ethnic group in Afghanistan. They are located in the southwestern part of the country. They speak Dari. Some also speak Pushtu or Brahui and all belong to the sunni sect of Islam. There are an estimated 200,000 Brahuis in Afghanistan. The Brahuis are tenant farmers or hired herders for the Baluchs or the Pushtuns.
Farsiwan: About 600,000 agriculturalist Farsiwans live in western Afghanistan. They are not to be mistaken for the Tajiks. The Farsiwans speak Dari and are sunni Muslims.
Gujar: This is a herding-farming group located east of Nuristan. They speak Hindustani and Pushtu. They belong to the sunni sect of Islam.
Hazara: About 870,000 in number, they live in the Bamyan region. They are agriculturalists. Many have moved to Kabul for urban work. They speak

Hazaragi, a Dari dialect, and belong to the shi'a sect of Islam.

Hindu: About 20,000 live in urban centers, and are engaged as merchants and traders. They speak Hindi and often Pushtu or Dari. They practice Hinduism.

Jews: About ten thousand live in Kabul and other large cities. They are merchants or traders. They practice Judaism and speak Hebrew, Dari and/or Pushtu.

Kirghiz: Several thousand live in the Pamir Mountains. They lead a transhumant life. Their language is a Turkic dialect. The Kirghiz belong to the sunni sect of Islam.

Moghul: About 20,000 live in central and northern Afghanistan. They practice agriculture and farm labor. They speak Dari with some Mongolian words. They practice sunni Islam.

Nuristani: About 100,000 live in eastern Afghanistan. They were converted to Islam during the reign of Abdul Rahman Khan. They speak Pushtu and practice sunni Islam.

Sikh: Several thousand live in urban areas occupied as merchants and traders. They speak Hindi, Pushtu, and/or Dari. They practice sikhism.

Tajik: There are about four million Tajiks living in northern Afghanistan. They refer to themselves by the geographic area in which they live. They are predominantly sunni Muslims, although some belong to the shi'a sect. The majority of the Tajiks speak tajiki dialects, and the rest speak Dari.

Turkman: Some 125,000 sedentary and semi-nomadic Turkmans live in northern Afghanistan. They are famous for the Qaraqul sheep raising, and rug making. They speak a Turkic dialect and practice sunni Islam.

Uzbek: About one million sedentary and agriculturist Uzbeks live in northern Afghanistan. They speak Turkic dialects and belong to the sunni sect of Islam.

EXTENDED FAMILY. A variation of the family found in Afghanistan where a domestic group consisting of three (or possibly more) generations of related individuals, including one or more marital groups in each of two adjacent generations, live together or very close to each other. It is usually formed when a young man, after marriage, brings his wife to live with him at, or very close to, his father's household. The extended family is found throughout rural Afghanistan and in major portions of the urban population.

-F-

FAIZABAD. Capital of Badakhshan Province. The town is located about 60 miles from Qunduz. Faizabad, like most other provincial capitals, can be reached by air directly from Kabul. The town is located on the banks of the Kokcha River. Faizabad is a thriving capital with crowded bazaars and many new buildings planned or in the making.

FAKHRUDDIN RAZI. A well-known theologian of the 12th century. The Friday Mosque in Herat was rebuilt in his memory by Sultan Ghia Suddin Ghori in 1200 A.D. The teachings of Razi were a great influence on the literary circles during his time.

FARAH (CITY). Capital of Farah Province. Farah is a small town bypassed by the western highway. There are plans to connect the city via a new paved road with the major East-West trunk highway, making it more accessible to both Herat and Qandahar, as well as to the rest of Afghanistan.

FARAH (PROVINCE). The largest province in Afghanistan, Farah is located in the southwest part of the country. It has an area of 59,590 sq. km., and its capital is Farah. Rug and carpet weaving is very important to the province. Because of a lack of irrigation and farm equipment there are many arid plains on which the sheep and goats, producing the wool for weaving, graze. Villagers noted for their skill at weaving these carpets are those of

Farah Rud River

Shindand, Khake, Safid, Qali Kah, and Anar Dara.

FARAH RUD RIVER. This river rises in the Siah Koh Mountains about 160 miles north of Qandahar. It follows a 350 mile course southwest and finally empties into the Hamun-i-Sabari, the northwest lagoon of the Hamun-i-Helmand Lake, a large marshy lake near the Iranian frontier. See also SEISTAN BASIN.

FARIAB (PROVINCE). A province located in the northwest area of Afghanistan. It has an area of 21,030 sq. km. and its capital is Maimana. Fariab is particularly noted for the quality of its horsemen who play buzkashi (see GAMES AND SPORTS). The chapandazes or horsemen from this area who play buzkashi are most often the outstanding players in the buzkashi games held in Kabul. Horses are important economically as the care and training of them provides jobs for hundreds of people. Raising of cereals and cotton is important in this province, as is the livestock--most especially Qaraqul sheep. Carpet weaving and the sale of these is very important economically, particularly in Daulatabad Woloswali and Andkhoi. Qaraqul cooperatives now organized in the country are a great aid to livestock breeders.

FARROKHI OF SEISTAN. A sensitive and powerful poet who lived during the Ghaznavid period.

FARSI see LANGUAGES

FARSIWAN. An Afghan who speaks Farsi. (Dari is the most recent name given to Farsi.) See also ETHNIC GROUPS.

FAUNA AND FLORA. The variations in flora and fauna of Afghanistan are expressions of the wide range of variability in the geography and climate of the country. The most common domesticated animals include horses, donkeys, mules, camels, sheep, goats, cattle, water buffalo, yaks, chickens, turkeys, dogs, and cats. Wild animals and birds are also found. Frequently found are wild goats and sheep, deer, gazelles, wolves, foxes, and jackals. Hares and rodents, mainly mice, abound. Other wild animals include the snow leopard, macaques (in Nuristan), ibex, wildcat, hyena, leopard, jungle cat, mongoose, otter, badgers, wild pig, markhor, Marco Polo sheep, and red deer. Snakes, including some venomous species, are found everywhere. Lizards are common, as are iguanas. The rivers of Afghanistan offer a wide variety of fish, including trout. Crickets are prevalent in the oases. Grasshoppers are very common. Some venomous spiders and scorpions occur, particularly in the dry and arid areas. Migratory birds, including ducks, are common. Pheasants are rare, but the quail stock is abundant. Other birds found in Afghanistan include partridge, lark, sparrow, flamingo, bustard, dove, pigeon, hawk, falcon, vulture, and nightingale.

The flora (vegetation) of Afghanistan is as varied as its faunal varieties. Pine and fir forests are found in the highest mountains. Cedar is abundant at altitudes of about 5,500 and 7,200 feet. Below this altitude oak is prevalent. Juniper forests are also found. Other trees include willows, wild olive, and birch. Sugarcane grows in the mountainous warm valleys of east and south Afghanistan. Date palms are common in the southwest region around Farah and Qandahar. Cereal plants include barley, wheat, rye, millet, rice, and castor oil plants. Fruit and nut trees include apricot, pear, apple, walnut, peach, mulberry, almond, quince, plum, grape, pomegranate, orange, lemon, fig, date, and banana. Vegetables and other plants include garden peas, broad beans, radishes, flax, alfalfa, opium poppies, lentils, clover, carrots, cucumbers, mustard, tobacco, potatoes, chick peas, pumpkins, melons, fennel, vetch, sunflowers, Zanzibar peas, oleaster, watermelons, artichokes, sesame, beets, spinach, salad greens, cabbage, garlic, leek, tomatoes, cherries, pine nuts, strawberries, asparagus, turnips, brussel sprouts, eggplant, lettuce, cauliflower, and squash.

FEBETCHENKO. Reportedly the second largest glacier in the world, found in the Pamir Mountains in the northeastern province of Badakhshan. Seventy-five kilometers long and between 500 and 600 meters thick, this glacier and others are the sources of many of Asia's rivers.

FIROZ KOH MOUNTAINS   see   GEOGRAPHY

FIVE PILLARS OF ISLAM. The Universal Five Pillars of Islam practiced among the Muslims of Afghanistan are:

1. Testimony to the Oneness of Allah (God).
2. Five times daily prayer.   See DAILY PRAYERS.
3. Alms giving.   See ZAKAT.
4. Fasting from sunrise to sunset during the month of Ramadzan (q.v.).
5. Haj (q.v.).   Pilgrimage to Mecca at least once in a Muslim's lifetime, if he/she can afford it.

FLAG. The flag of the Republic of Afghanistan has a rectangular form, the longer sides of which are one and one-half times the length of the shorter sides. The colors of the flag are black, green, and red which run horizontally from one small side to the other small side. The black color (symbolizing Afghan history and past) appears uppermost. Its width is one-fourth of the width of the flag. Below the black strip is the red color (symbolizing the valor and the sacrifices of the people of Afghanistan) which appears in the same proportion as the black strip. Below the red appears the green color (symbolizing an atmosphere of tranquility, hope, and prosperity created by the Republic of Afghanistan as well as the progress and development of the state and people of Afghanistan), the width of which is one-half the width of the flag. The Afghan national emblem is imprinted in the top corner of the flag.

FLETCHER, ARNOLD. An American historian who has spent much time in Afghanistan and written substantively about the history of Afghanistan. See also Bibliography.

FOLK MUSIC. Like many dimensions of the Afghan cultural and ethnic varieties, folk music and instruments contain features of Central Asia, Iran, and the Indian subcontinent. Some cultural continuity appears to exist among the highland societies of Eurasia from the Carpathians and the Balkans to the Hindu Kush, and possibly the western end of the Himalayas. Many poems, both oral and written, have been set to music, but variations exist from region to region and from performer(s) to performer(s), who improvise, add, and/or delete, as the context and situation dictates. See also MUSICAL INSTRUMENTS.

FOOD. The staples of the Afghan diet are wheat, rice, meat, vegetables, fruits, and oil. Many variations in the cooking and preparation of rice exist. The widely used general term for a rice dish is palaw. Often coloring, fruits, and nuts are added to cooked rice. Vegetables are either eaten raw as a salad or stewed alone or with chunks of lamb meat. Although lamb meat has the widest consumption, beef, poultry, venison, goat, and camel meat are also eaten. Nomads are the largest consumers of camel meat. Dairy products, such as milk, cheese, and yoghurt, are frequent supplements of the Afghan diet. All meat must be slaughtered according to set rituals and procedures spelled out in Islamic dicta. Beverages include black and green tea, colas and sodas (in cities and major towns), and a popular drink called dogh (in Dari) and shromby (in Pushtu). Dogh or shromby is watered-down yoghurt with pieces of cucumber and mint.

Afghanistan is known for its many varieties of fruits. Melons and grapes have both the widest variety and consumption. (There are an estimated eighty varieties of grapes alone.) The best varieties of melon are produced in the north and northwest. Grapes, melons, and other fruits often supplement Afghan food. Grapes and melons are also exported in large quantities. Dried fruits such as raisins, apricots, and a variety of nuts are also consumed, especially during the winter months. In parts of Afghanistan, mulberries are ground and dried into cakes and are eaten with nuts during winter. Dried mulberries are called <u>talkhan</u>. Meat is also dried (landy) for consumption during the winter months. Other popular foods include varieties of Kababs, bread-dough stuffed with meat and/or vegetables and fried (bulani), steamed, or boiled (<u>ashak</u>). Pastries and sweets are also eaten as snacks or with meals. See also FAUNA AND FLORA.

FRIDAY MOSQUE   see   MASJIDE JAME

FRUITS   see   FAUNA AND FLORA

-G-

GADI. A two-wheeled, horsedrawn carriage commonly found in large Afghan towns and cities. It is primarily used for the transport of passengers. The modern taxi is rapidly replacing the Gadi. In some larger cities such as Kabul, the Gadi is prohibited from central city streets or roads. With the increasing advent of bus and taxi service, Gadi service is destined to disappear in the very near future.

GAMES AND SPORTS. The most famous sport in Afghanistan, and one of the world's roughest, is the game of <u>buzkashi</u>, which is played with a beheaded calf or a goat and with teams of horsemen called chapandaz. The number of players may vary from 10 to 500 on each side. The object of the game is to snatch the carcass from a shallow ditch, around which a circle has been marked, and to carry it outside an enormous field, round a given point at the far end, and to return and fling it back in the original circle. At the start, the riders make a dash for the carcass. The man who picks it up after an exciting struggle flings it across his saddle and goes off at full gallop, while others chase him closely until one of them (a member of the opposite team) catches up with him. The struggle between the two riders for possession of the carcass is fierce. Often the carcass falls and other riders make a grab for it. The team which eventually manages to return it to the ditch in the circle is declared the winner. Buzkashi requires intricate skills of horsemanship, coordination, and above all teamwork. The game is primarily a Central Asian sport and belongs properly in the so-called "horse-culture" tradition of the traditions of Central Asia. Thus, it is not surprising that buzkashi is exclusively played by the ethnic groups of northern Afghanistan.

In most Afghan games and sports zan, zar, and zameen (women, gold, and land) are the organizing principles. The desire for the possession and/or control of these units is symbolically woven into games and recreational activities. Kite flying, tup dandah (a game combining elements of cricket and stickball), chub dandah (played by young boys), and various card games are popular. Cockfighting, larkfighting, and partridge fighting are common throughout Afghanistan. Ram fighting is also common. Game birds, such as ducks and partridge, are frequently hunted. Large game hunting includes wild sheep, goats, gazelles, snow leopards, and bears.

Wrestling, tugging, swimming, mountain climbing, fishing, and trapping of birds and animals are popular indigenous sports in Afghanistan. Western sports such as soccer, field hockey, volleyball, tennis, weightlifting, boxing, and basketball are played primarily in urban areas, particularly in formal schools--high schools and universities. With the exception of buzkashi and wrestling, there are no professional sports in Afghanistan.

Afghan Hounds (tazi) abound in Afghanistan. Shorter haired and longer headed than their counterparts in the West, the tazi, indigenous to

Afghanistan, are highly regarded among the Afghans. They are used for hunting. Some tazi have been clocked at fifty miles an hour.
See also DURA BAZI.

GANDHARA. A historical reference to an area which includes the present provinces of Kabul, Jalalabad, and some regions immediately to the eastern border of Afghanistan. Also a particular art style which combines both Buddhic and popular art styles is characteristic of this region.

GARDAIZ. Capital of Pakthia Province. A small town in the heart of the Pushtun area. There is a Buddhic archaeological site near the town. Gardaiz played an important strategic role in the conquest of Kabul by King Mohammed Nadir Khan. The town is accessible through secondary roads and by airline.

GARDEZI. A prosaic chronicler who lived during the Ghaznavid period.

GAUTAMA BUDDHA (563-483 B.C.) (SIDDHARTHA). The son of Suddhodana, a Raja, he enjoyed a very pleasurable life. He married Yasodharma, a beautiful woman, and had a son. Though very prosperous, he could be satisfied by nothing. Eventually he left his home and family and spent several years in meditation attempting to ascertain the meaning of life. This resulted in his becoming the "Enlightened One"--(Buddha). He then traveled widely preaching this necessity for striving for Nirvana, the abode of eternal peace. He is considered the teacher-incarnation of Vishnu. See also HISTORY--Buddhist Period.

GENGHIZ KHAN see CHENGIS KHAN

GEOGRAPHY. From the point of view of total ecology, emphasizing channels of human contact and communication in reference to zones of accessibility and relative inaccessibility, the geographic zones of Afghanistan can best be divided into the following major zones:

<u>Central Highlands</u>: Afghanistan's mountainous core, the Central Highlands, is part of the great Alpine-Himalayan mountain range. An intricate interwoven pattern of ridges and valleys, the Central Highlands extend over an area of approximately 160,000 square miles. The mountains emanate out of the Pamir Knot in the east toward Iran in the west and enclose several arid plateaus. Transverse ridges point toward the Northern Plains; the southern ranges cross over the eastern border of Afghanistan.

The aproximately east-west mountain axis is composed of three high ridges with the altitudes descending toward Iran. The main ridge begins in China and runs southwestward about 300 miles at the Eastern Hindu Kush with peaks over 21,000 feet high, and mountain passes at altitudes between 12,000 and 15,000 feet. At 13,000 feet Anjuman Pass, in the Eastern Hindu Kush, is the portal to the Central Hindu Kush. The former is a cold desert highland with snow covered peaks and practically no vegetation. Flanked by huge, longitudinal valleys, the highest crest (16,650 feet) of the Central Hindu Kush is just west of the important Salang Pass (11,000 feet) on the main road from Kabul to the Northern Plains.

The Kohe Baba Range with peaks at 15,000 feet runs parallel to and south of the western end of the Central Hindu Kush, to which it is connected by two transverse ridges. Together with the Hindu Kush, the Kohe Baba extend westward and constitute the country's main watershed. Several smaller ranges spring out of the Hindu Kush and Kohe Baba and extend north and south.

<u>Northern Plains</u>: North of the central mountain core are the Northern Plains, stretching from the Iranian border to the western foothills of the Pamir Knot. The area, part of the Central Asian Steppe, is demarcated on its eastern half from the Soviet

Union by the Amu Darya River. Extending over an area of approximately 40,000 square miles, the Northern Plains are situated at an average elevation of 2,000 feet except for the Amu Darya valley floor where it drops to as low as 600 feet. A considerable portion of the area consists of fertile, loess-covered plains. Intensely cultivated and densely settled, these plains are of major agricultural importance and provide food for a considerable portion of Afghanistan's population. They also have rich natural gas resources.

The Southwestern Plateau: This area, situated southwest of the Central Highlands, is a high arid plateau extending beyond the eastern and western boundaries of Afghanistan. With an altitude of about 3,000 feet, it slopes gently to the southwest. Comprised of deserts and semi-deserts, it is crossed by a few large rivers among which the Helmand and Arghandab are the most important. The region covers approximately 50,000 square miles, a fourth of which forms the Registan Desert. Agriculture is most intense along the banks of the major rivers and their smaller tributaries.

GHAZNAVID DYNASTY see HISTORY--Ghaznavid
    Period

GHAZNI (CITY). Capital of Ghazni Province. Ghazni is located about 85 miles southwest of Kabul, and about 220 miles northeast of Qandahar. It is an important market city, and is famous for the embroidered sheepskin and foxskin coats (posteens). The rapidly expanding Ghazni lies at the base of an important ruined citadel beside the Ghazni River. Ghazni was a major Buddhist center during the 7th century A.D. The city was conquered by Islamic armies during the mid 9th century A.D. Ghazni later became the capital of the great Ghaznavi empire (994-1160 A.D.). At its zenith the city was the center of major educational institutions and splendid architecture. The tomb of Mahmood Ghaznavi is located in Ghazni along with

Ghazni (Province)

the shrines of other famous poets and sufis of the Ghaznavid period. The city was burned and razed in 1151 A.D. by the Ghorid Sultan, Ala-u-Din Jahansuz (Ala-u-Din, the world burner). After recovering from this holocaust, the city was once again totally destroyed by Chengis Khan in 1221 A.D.

GHAZNI (PROVINCE). A province located in the southwest area of Afghanistan. It has an area of 31,106 sq. km. and ranks 9th in size among the provinces. Its capital is Ghazni. Several dams are used to irrigate the land for farming. Important products include wheat, barley, corn, flax, and sesame. Sheepskin jackets called "posteenchas" (waist-high posteens) with intricate embroidery work on them are well-known. Rug making is important and major centers include Moqor, Jaghory, and Malestan. This province has a rich history, particularly during the years from 963 A.D. to 1186 A.D. when literature and architectural styles flourished. Ruins of Buddhist monasteries dating to the 7th century have also been found.

GHAZNI BASIN. Formed by the Ghazni and Nahoor Rivers. The Ghazni River rises in southwest Ghazni and flows for about ninety miles until it empties into Abe-Istada, 1,968 meters above sea level. The Nahoor River is sixty miles in length and it also empties into Abe-Istada Lake. Its catchment area is 660 square miles.

GHAZNI RIVER see GHAZNI BASIN

GHILZAI DYNASTY.
Mir Wais Hotak	1709-1715
Abdul Aziz Hotak	1715-1719
Shah Mahmood Hotak	1719-1725
Shah Ashraf Hotak (in Isfahan)	1725-1729
Shah Husain Hotak (in Qandahar)	1725-1738

GHILZAI TRIBES. These Pushtun tribes are located primarily on both sides of the east and southeastern borders of Afghanistan. The major Ghilzai tribes include: hotak, tokhi, sulaymankhayl, andar, nasir, ahmadzai, alikhayl, wazir, mangal, zadran, kharoti, shinwari, afridi, khugiani, mangal, taraki, shinwari, jaji, yusufzai, momand, jabarkhayl, and safi.

GHOR (PROVINCE). A province located in the west-central portion of Afghanistan. It ranks 7th in size among Afghan provinces. Its capital is Chaghcharan. Some wheat and barley are grown, but due to the climate and generally poor soil, only one crop per year is possible, and often the soil must be allowed to "rest" every other year. During the summers farmers often move to their fields and live in chaparis (q.v.) which they erect. The mountains in this province--the Bayan Range--are the source of most of the rivers of western Afghanistan--the Murghab to the north, the Hari Rud to the west, and Farah Rud to the southwest. Dura Bazi (q.v.) or whip racing is a popular sport. Many archaeological ruins may be found in the Bayan range. Interesting sites are: the Qalai Qaisar, started by Sultan Alauddin and finished by Sultan Ghiasuddin; Kalai Sangi, a 12th century Ghorid city; and one in Fermis Alakadari.

GHUBAR, G. A prominent contemporary Afghan historian who has written extensively on Afghan history. His scholarly works are the most original contributions provided by a native Afghan historiographer.

GHUR see **GHOR (PROVINCE)**

GHURID DYNASTY. The Ghurids, believed to be the descendants of earlier Turkic speaking people, lived in the mountains of Ghor. They ascended to dominance over Afghanistan after the Ghaznavid rulers. The Ghaznavids established their rule over India with their political capital in Ghazni.

They won decisive battles over the Indians, and ruled the subcontinent over a period of time. Their most distinguished ruler in Afghanistan and in India is Sultan Mahmood Ghaznavi.

GHWARI see ROGHAN ZARD

GIRISHK see HELMAND RIVER and HELMAND VALLEY

GREAT FRIDAY MOSQUE OF HERAT. A magnificent piece of architecture, dating to the time of the Ghurids. It still stands and has been recently repaired--a fitting monument to the Ghurids, who were great builders and patrons of art and learning. It was built by Sultan Ghiassud Din in the 12th century A. D.

GREAT NORTH ROAD. A paved highway which connects Kabul with the Afghan-Russian border port of Qizil Qala on the Amu Darya. It was blasted out of solid rock through the heart of the Himalayas--reaching altitudes of over 3,000 meters. It was built recently under a contract between the Ministry of Public Works of Afghanistan and the Institute of Techno-Export of the Soviet Union. It shortens the former distance between its beginning and end by 200 kilometers.

GUJAR. A small tribal group of mountaineers who occupy the eastern border of Afghanistan. The Gujars are sheep- and goat-herding farmers. They are also involved in raising livestock and are known for their production of dairy products. Although they are Muslims, Islam has not penetrated the cultural/ethnic plane of the Gujars as it has in many other areas of Afghanistan.

GUR (GURA in Pushtu). A term for a black or brown variety of sugar which is made out of the juice of sugar cane.

-H-

HADDA. An archaeological site located five miles south of Jalalabad. An important Buddhist monastery center and a famous place for pilgrims to visit, it dates from the 2nd to the 6th centuries. Fahien, a 5th century Chinese pilgrim, and Hiuantsang, a 7th century Chinese pilgrim, refer to this place. Among those who have undertaken archaeological excavation here are: M. Godard, M. Foucher, and M. Barthoux (all in the 1920's).
    Hellenistic art seems to have had noticeable influence at Hadda, as did medieval Romanesque and Gothic art of Western European Christianity.

HADITH. Part of the sharia, the Islamic code of conduct and law. The Hadith refers to the verified sayings of the Prophet Mohammed.

HAJ. One of the five tenets of Islam, it requires all Muslims to make a pilgrimage to Mecca at least once in their lifetime, if they can afford it. See also FIVE PILLARS OF ISLAM.

HAJI. A person who, as a Muslim, has made the pilgrimage to Mecca. A Haji, upon fulfillment of this tenet of Islam, becomes a respected leader in his community. In Afghanistan the Hajis are looked up to for advice, guidance, and often leadership.

HAKEEM. Hakeems (derived from the Arabic term meaning "wise") are much respected traditional folk-medical practitioners. They prescribe treatments and remedies originally expounded in century-old Persian and Arabic medical texts. Some of the treatments and remedies provided by the Hakeems are occasionally effective.

HAKEEM SANAI. A native of Ghazni born in the second half of the 11th century and who died between

1140-1150 A. D. He was a well-known Sufi poet
of the Ghaznavid period. He is considered one
of the three great mystic poets of Persian literature. He began as a panegyrist and held an important position at the Ghaznavid court. Later he
spent all of his time and energy in meditation and
the composing of mystic poetry. One of his "students," Maulana Jalaluddin Rumi (q.v.) is also
among the three best known mystic poets.

HAMMAM. A community bath with hot and cold running
water. Every large Afghan town and all Afghan
cities have a Hammam. Often a Hamman will
have some private rooms equipped with water taps.
Men and women use these baths at alternate times
of the day or on alternate days.

HAMUN-I-HELMAND LAKE. A huge salty, marshy
lake which expands and contracts in relation to
the flow of the rivers from season to season. It
lies at the Iranian frontier and supports a marsh-
dwelling people who subsist on fish and wildfowl.
This lake is fed by the Farah Rud and the Helmand
Rivers. Over half of the land area of Afghanistan
drains into the southwest basin, and eventually into
this lake.

HANAFI. One of the four Islamic schools of jurisprudence. The other three are Hanbali, Miliki, and
Shafi'ai. The Hanafi school of law is operative
in Afghanistan, thus making it mandatory that Islamic religious rites in the country be performed
according to the provisions of this school of Islamic law and jurisprudence.

HANBALI   see   HANAFI

HARAVATI   see   QANDAHAR

HARI RUD RIVER. This river, which rises in the
mountains of central Afghanistan, has watersheds
in the Paropamisus mountains and the western
range of the Hindu Kush. It flows from east to

west as far as the village of Kahson and then turns north and for 90 km. forms the boundary between Afghanistan and Iran. Tributaries of the Hari Rud are the Kawgan (260 km.) and the Korrukh (98 km.).
The Hari Rud and its tributaries disappear in the Turkaman desert. The catchment area of the basin is 1,720 sq. km.
It eventually enters Turkmenistan, a Soviet Socialist Republic, and ends in the Kara-Kum desert near the town of Tedzhen. See also HERAT BASIN and RIVERS.

HASAN MAIMANDI. A poet during the Ghaznavid period who described the "great civilization" in poetic style. He was from Maimandi (which is now Maiwand, near Bost).

HAZARA see ETHNIC GROUPS

HAZARAJAT. A rugged, sparsely populated area located in the central part of Afghanistan where the Hindu Kush breaks up into several separate chains. The Hazara tribes living here use what pasture there is for grazing their stock.

HELMAND (PROVINCE). This is the third largest of the Afghan provinces. Located in the southwestern part of the country, Helmand province is an agricultural area with wheat, cotton, and barley as the main crops. Fruits, particularly grapes, are widely grown. One of the largest dams and hydroelectric projects is built on the Helmand River, which runs from the northeast part of the province to the southwest. Plans are in the making for further irrigation projects and for industrial development. See also HELMAND VALLEY.

HELMAND-ARGHANDAB VALLEY AUTHORITY (HAVA). A huge irrigation and hydroelectric project on the Helmand and Arghandab Rivers. It was begun in the early 1950's and is in the last phases of its completion. The project under the supervision of the Helmand-Arghandab River Authority, is designed for the settlements of nomads and for the irrigation of the previously arid lands in southwestern Afghanistan.

HELMAND RIVER. This 700-mile river is the longest river entirely within the country of Afghanistan. It begins its course in the western Paghman Mountains and follows a southwesterly direction through the Hazarajat region into the southern plains at Girishk. Part of the river is diverted here by an irrigation dam to feed the system based on the Baghra Canal. It then flows between the Registan on the east and the Dasht-i-Margo on the west and at Qala Bist, it is joined by the Arghandab, Tarnak and Arghastan Rivers. The Helmand ultimately empties into the Seistan lacustrine depression in the south. See also SEISTAN BASIN.

HELMAND VALLEY. Located in the province of Helmand, this valley is extremely important economically to the entire area. Two major rivers, the Arghandab and Helmand, which cross this valley, have provided the opportunity for the irrigation of land as well as power plants. During the late 1930's work began on developing the Valley. The Boghra Canal near Girishk was rebuilt as the initial phase of the project. By 1966 the project included power production and reclaiming land by irrigation as well as settling nomads. Consumer industries were started and modern agricultural methods were taught and put into practice.

A long-term credit agreement signed with the United States in July, 1965 will be used to build the Kajaki power plant which initially will generate 60,000 kilowatts of power for Qandahar and Helmand. Eventually it will produce over 100,000 kilowatts of power for industry in western Afghanistan.

HERAT. Capital of Herat Province, this city profoundly reflects the cultural traditions of Iran, Central Asia, and others within Afghanistan. The city, with a population of 85,000, is about 660 miles from Kabul via Qandahar, and accessible by paved highways and regular air service. Many ethnic groups, representing the cultural mosaic of Afghanistan, are represented in Herat. The city has a distinguished political, artistic, and literary history. New large and numerous small hotels are available in Herat, as well as a variety of restaurants. Herat, located on the Hari Rud River, draws large numbers of tourists throughout the year. Herat was originally built by Alexander the Great and its political and economic control shifted many times from one ruling dynasty to another over a period of several centuries. Many historic ruins can be found within and near the present city. The Great Friday Mosque of Herat is one of the best architectural examples of the Timurid period. Grapes, cherries, and melons are grown in surrounding areas as are cotton, wheat, rice, and alfalfa.

HERAT (PROVINCE). The sixth largest province of Afghanistan, Herat is one of the most fertile agricultural regions in the country. Industry and production are on the increase. The Hari Rud River runs from east to west, dividing the province into north and south regions. The banks of the Hari Rud River and its tributaries are among the most densely populated agricultural areas in Afghanistan. The province of Herat abounds in historic and prehistoric archaeological sites. The grapes and melons of Herat are the most famous in the country. The majority of the population of Herat are Tajik and Dari speaking groups.

HERAT BASIN. The main course of this basin is formed by the Hari Rud River. Tributaries include the Kawgan (about 40 miles) and the Korrukh (about 40 miles). The waters of these rivers are very important to the agricultural area south of Herat.

HIJRA. The journey which took Prophet Mohammed

from Mecca to Medina in 613 A.D. is called Hijra. The lunar year of Islam begins with the day Prophet Mohammed began this journey.

HINAYANA (BUDDHISM). The Southern School of Buddhism meaning, literally, "the Smaller Wheel." It looks towards Buddha as an enlightened one, an inspired teacher, who preached the middle path between indulgence and asceticism. It was not a religion, but a philosophy of life and a code of morals. Buddha was depicted, not in human form, but by "an empty chair, a footprint, an umbrella, a riderless horse, or even an empty throne." See MAHAYANA BUDDHISM.

HINDU see ETHNIC GROUPS

HINDU KUSH MOUNTAINS. The Hindu Kush extends 800 km. northeast to southwest. Its origin is in the Pamir Mountains and it is an extension of the Himalaya Mountains. It is the backbone of Afghanistan and abounds in fertile valleys and rivers. It divides the country into two areas: the valleys of the north, flat and fertile, most suitable for agriculture; and the rocky southern section, heavily forested and rich in timber. Some of its northern spurs are important and a number of peaks are over 15,000 feet high. Glaciers cut through numerous passes.

The most important passes of this range are:

The Baroghil	12,460 feet
The Dorah	14,900 feet
The Khawak	11,460 feet
The Khaknoll	3,400 feet
The Thull	3,600 feet
The Salang	11,100 feet
The Koashan	14,900 feet
The Shibar	10,779 feet
The Dandan Shikan	10,500 feet
The Unai	10,827 feet
The Hajigak	12,140 feet

Based on present knowledge, it seems that

the Hindu Kush emerged in Paleozoic times, and
was covered at the end of the era by the waters
of the Permean period. The Mesozoic era saw
the mass rise again and then submerge until, during the Cenozoic era, it assumed its present form.
    Frequent earthquakes and tremors are
caused by an extension of a branch of the Pacific
earthquake belt from the Himalayas into the Hindu
Kush. The highest peak in the range is the
Tirich Mir which rises to 25,263 feet. It is located in the southwest of the Wakhan corridor.
The main chain, which extends toward the west
from the Hindu Kush, is the Paropamisus Range,
which ends near the Iranian frontier. The Kohe
Baba is thrown off to the south in the heart of the
country. See also GEOGRAPHY.

HISTORY.

Indo-Aryans. It was about 2,000 B.C. when a
group of Aryans for the first time took to a sedentary life, building cities and towns, and setting up
a government and so on. One of the most important towns which they founded was Bakhdium Sariram
Ordovo Darafsham or Balkh (q.v.), the beautiful
city of high flags.
    Hymns in the Rig Veda give the earliest
references to the area now known as Afghanistan.
It has an abundance of geographical and other data.
    The Avesta, which became the Holy Book of
the Iranians, calls the part of Asia, which is now
Afghanistan, "Aryana." From here the "Aryans,"
the common ancestors of the oldest Iranians and
Indians, emerged. The Avesta and the Rig Veda
contain many of the same terms for common concepts and names of divinities. The prophet Zoroaster was an important figure during this time.

Achaemenids. The first historical evidence of
foreign intervention (as distinguished from tribal
migrations) is around 600 B.C. Cyrus the Great
(549-529 B.C.) and Darius I (522-485 B.C.) took
control of many parts of the country. Darius I

went as far as the Indus Valley and West Punjab.
Greek writers were now able to visit Afghanistan.
The Persians had considerable influence and even
after the 4th century B.C., when their control
relaxed, many areas still carried their mark--in
solar cults, the idea of divine monarchy, in architecture, i.e., in the pillars and lion capitals of
Ashoka, the Mauryan King, etc.

Greeks (Graeco-Bactrian Kingdom). Beginning in
330 B.C. Alexander the Great invaded and defeated
the Achaemenids. He then proceeded on to Aryana.
Alexandria Ariorum was founded near what is today
Herat. He then continued to Bactria. Greek
colonists for two centuries (300 to 100 B.C.)
maintained a Hellenized culture in Central Asia
marked by oriental and local traits. After the
death of Alexander in 323 B.C., the Seleucus
monarchy took control of what is now Iran and
Afghanistan. Seleucus I Nicator ruled Bactria
from 311 B.C. In 250 B.C. the independence of
Bactria was proclaimed and Diodotus I founded a
line of twenty-nine kings and three queens. This
was known as the Graeco-Bactrian Kingdom. A
great city from this period has been uncovered
near Ai-Khanum, at the confluences of the Kokcha
and Oxus Rivers.

Invasions from the north by the Parthians,
a Saka tribe, and the Yueh-Chih in about 130 B.C.
brought new power and influence to the area.

Buddhist Period. The Kushans (one of the Yueh-
Chih clans) established its power and ruled during
the first several centuries A.D. They united
Bactria and Sogdiana, defeated the Parthians and
the Sakas in the west, extended their rule over
the Kabul Valley and Kashmir to the south, and
later continued to expand their domain as far as
Benares in India. The two important dynasties
were the Kadphises and the Kanishkas.

King Kanishka (q.v.) of the 1st or 2nd century A.D. is a famous reformer of the Buddhist
religion. Mahayana ("the great Vehicle") was the

name of the division of the Buddhist faith which he codified.

A center at this time was Kapisa. It was part of the caravan route ("Soil Route") from Antioch on the Mediterranean to Bactria, Kapisa, Hadda, and Peshawar. A northern route went from Bactria toward China. Southwest Asia continued to be opened to the influence of Greek civilization and Greek art. Greek realism, syncretized with Indian spiritualism and the Graeco-Buddhist Art of Gandhara, or Gandhara School of Art, resulted.

From the 3rd century A.D. onwards, Kushan power declined and Kabul and neighboring areas were invaded by the Sassanians and later the White Huns (Ephthalites). Monasteries were destroyed, and the fierce attacks destroyed countless people. It was indeed a period of great upheaval. The Arabs did not conquer all of Afghanistan, but their incursion carried enough influence so that Islam gradually made inroads into the country. It has been an important factor in Afghan life since that time.

Islamic Period. The 7th century brought Arab armies into Afghanistan and soon after this the Islamic religion had converts throughout the country. Leaders of the country began to recognize the authority of the Caliph at Baghdad. The 9th century found the Taharids in power. One of their military governors, Yaqub ibn Layth, set up his own area of power (an area which included most of what is today modern Afghanistan). The Saffarid Dynasty lost its power at the beginning of the 10th century and another dynasty--the Samanids --took control.

Ismail reigned at this time (892-907 A.D.). This was an important period of time in the cultural life of the country. Bokhara, the capital, became a center of learning. Important poets of the time include Rodaki, who was the important lyric poet, and Daqiqi of Balk who was well-known for his epic poetry, particularly his

depictions of the great deeds of the ancient kings.
The important philosopher was Ibn-Sina (Avicenna)
who revived Aristotelian science in the Orient.
He benefitted greatly from the excellent library,
which had been collected at Bokhara by the Samanids. A school of writers and scholars began to
grow.

Ghaznavid Period. One of the more important of
the dynasties in Afghan history was the Ghaznavid
Dynasty founded in 962 by Alptigin (Alptegin). A
great cultural center grew in Ghazni and upwards
of four hundred historians, scientists, and poets
lived here. During this period the country's summer capital was Ghazni and the winter capital was
Bost (Lashkar-gah) in southwestern Afghanistan.
Alptigin's successor was Sabuktagin, who extended
his power to Kabul. His son Mahmood succeeded
him and ruled from about 997 to 1030. He was
a very successful ruler and during the course of
numerous campaigns he extended his empire to
include the regions of the Hindu Kush, the Punjab
in India, and vast territory beyond the Oxus River,
meanwhile accumulating great wealth. This now
famous and wealthy kingdom was destroyed by
Alauddin of the Ghor, a mountainous region in
northwest Afghanistan.

Alauddin set fire to the capital of the
Ghaznavids and earned the title of "World Burner"
--Jahansooz. His nephew, Muizzuddin Mohammed,
invaded India in 1775 and established a sultanate
at Delhi. At about the same time, the Tajik
Souri tribe established the Shansabanid dynasty
at Bamyan. The Ghorid period of power held control until early in the 13th century. One of the
few remaining sites from this period is the
minaret of Jam (q.v.) near Chesht, east of Herat.
It was dedicated by Sultan Ghiasuddin (1153-1203).
It stands more than 60 meters tall and is composed of three transconical shafts on an octagonal
base.

Mongol Empire. The beginning of the 13th century

found Afghanistan under the rule of Sultan Alauddin Mohammed Khwarazmshah. He ruled an area including all the countries of Iraq in the west and the Indus in the southeast. As he was moving towards Baghdad in order to take even more territory, he was told of the advance of Chengis Khan (q.v.) and hordes of following Mongols. The Valley of the Amu Darya was invaded first and then Bamiyan, Balkh, Ghazni, and Herat were destroyed. The mass destruction of life and property wrought by these hordes is indescribable. It is believed by many that Afghanistan has never fully recovered from the incredible destruction of these times. Cities were burned and razed to the ground, canals destroyed, and with no irrigation networks, fields of crops became deserts.

The history of Afghanistan hereafter is divided as to person, event, or world area.

HOLIDAYS. Friday is the weekly holiday (literally, here, holy day) in Afghanistan. In 1970 the Afghan holidays (national, on solar calendar days, religious, on lunar calendar days) fell on the following days of the Gregorian calendar (note that the dates in the first column are given as points of time reference only. The date in the Gregorian calendar varies from year to year):

National Holidays:

March 21, 1970	Nawroz or New Year's Day, 1 day.
March 27, 1970	Independence Day, 1 day
August 31, 1970	Jeshn-i-Istiqlal or Independence Celebration, 3 days.
September 9, 1970	National Assembly Day, 1 day.
July 17, 1973	The Republic Day, 1 day.

Religious Holidays:

March 17, 1970	Moharram or Martyrs Day, 1 day.

May 17, 1970	Id-i-Milad, the Prophet's Birthday, 1 day.
October 30, 1970	1st of Ramadzan, month of fasting, 1 day.
November 29, 1970	Id-i-Fitr, end of Ramadzan, 3 days.
February 4, 1971	Id-i-Adha or Id-i-Qurban, day of sacrifice during the month of Haj, 4 days.

HOTAK see GHILZAI TRIBES

HUJRA see MELMASTIA

HYDROGRAPHY. The drainage network of Afghanistan is controlled by the structural form of its mountain ranges. See also KABUL BASIN, OXUS BASIN, HERAT BASIN, SEISTAN BASIN, and the GHAZNI BASIN.

-I-

IBN-SINA (980-1037). One of the greatest of Moslem philosophers. Born just north of the borders of modern Afghanistan, he revived Aristotelian science in the Orient. He benefited greatly from the library at Bukhara which had been collected by the Samanids.

ID-I-ADHA (ID-I-QURBAN). Sometimes called the "Big Id," it is a major ritual celebration with the sacrifice of an animal or some quantity of food. This is in commemoration of the period of Haj (q.v.), when pilgrims going to Mecca sacrifice animals memorializing the sacrificial offering of Ismael to God by his father Ibrahim (Abraham). The sacrificed meat is given to the poor and to close relatives. Much feasting takes place on this occasion among the Afghans.

ID-I-FITR. Sometimes called the "small Id," it is a

three-day period of festivities celebrating the end of the month of Ramadzan. Close friends and relatives visit with each other, much food is consumed, and Afghans display their best (new) clothes.

IMAM. Technically, any person who will lead a collective prayer. More commonly, the Imams lead Friday noon prayers. The status of the Imam can be interchangeable with that of the Mullah. See also MULLAH.

INDUSTRY see ECONOMY

INTERNATIONAL AIRPORTS see ARIANA AFGHAN AIRLINES

ISLAH. This bilingual daily newspaper began publication as a government controlled paper in the early 1930s. It is presently subsumed under the daily Jamhuryat. See also ANEES and JAMHURYAT.

ISLAM. One of the world's major religions. Islam is the dominant faith in Afghanistan. Islam provides a common spiritual bond among the country's diverse tribal and ethnic groups. Approximately 99 per cent of the people are Muslims, the great majority of whom adhere to the sunni sect of Islam. The shi'a sect comprises the remaining fraction of the Islamic population. Islam, as a faith and in practice, plays an important role in the Afghan Muslim's daily life. Moral and spiritual values are derived from Islam, shaping the Afghan's notions of ethical conduct, and the observance of its rituals are an integral part of his routine.
    The founder of Islam, Prophet Mohammed, was an Arab born about 570 A.D. at Mecca. At the age of about forty he began receiving revelations which he communicated to his disciples. He began preaching publicly at Mecca against the prevailing practices and beliefs, and earned the hostility of important leaders, who forced him to

migrate to Medina with his closest followers. From Medina he and his followers launched a series of campaigns to convert the nonbelievers and, ultimately, the entire Arabian peninsula came under their control. Mecca became the holy city of Islam.
Islam, literally, means submission to the will of Allah. Thus, in the traditional Islamic social order, religion and secular affairs have been intimately interwoven. See also FIVE PILLARS OF ISLAM AND HISTORY--Islamic Period.

ISTALIF. A small town about 15 miles north of Kabul, known for its scenery and for its unique blue-glazed pottery. Istalif is also a popular resort and picnicking area for tourists and the residents of Kabul.

IYLAQ. The high altitude pasturelands used by the nomads and herding groups for grazing. See also QISHLAQ.

-J-

JABUL SERAJ. A district in the province of Parwan which houses citadels and castles dating to the time of Alexander. Over fifty years ago, electricity was produced here to service Kabul and this area received it also. In the early 1960s a cement plant was brought in from Czechoslovakia and that industry began to gain importance.

JALALABAD. Capital of Nangarhar Province. It is located about 95 miles west of Kabul, and is accessible by road and air transport. Jalalabad is more or less a resort area for the urban Afghans, primarily from Kabul. There are many hotels and restaurants throughout the city. Jalalabad sits in an oasis ringed by mountains. Palaces, as well as large gardens and trees lining the avenues, speak of its long history as a royal winter capital. The warm climate during the winter months is the attraction for its many tourists. Located close to Jalalabad are many historical-archaeological sites. The most important of these sites in Hadda (q.v.), a large Buddhic historic site which has been excavated.

JAM MINARET. A magnificent minaret, near Chesht, east of Herat, which was dedicated by Sultan Ghiasuddin Ghuri (1153-1203). It is the sole remains of the Ghurid capital of Ferz Kohal. It consists of three transconical shafts on an octagonal base, reaching a height of over 60 meters. Bricks and stucco in geometric design, with kufic script as an ornament, give it a rich, decorative pattern.

JAMHURYAT. A bilingual (Dari and Pushtu) daily newspaper published in Kabul. Jamhuryat replaced the joint Anees/Islah daily newspapers after Afghanistan was proclaimed a republic in July, 1973. See also ANEES and ISLAH.

JAMI, NURUDDIN ABDURRAHMAN. One of the greatest 15th century poets. "Baharistan," the "Golden Chain," and the "Breezes of Affection" are among the best known of his 50 works which ranged from lives of the mystics to lyric poetry. A pistachio tree in the city of Herat marks his grave.

JAST. A Nuristani term for Malik. See also MALIK.

JERIB. A unit of land, common throughout Afghanistan. It is the equivalent of approximately 0.5 acres.

JESHN (CELEBRATION OF AFGHAN INDEPENDENCE). In all provincial capitals of Afghanistan, this event is celebrated over a three-day period--a time filled with great activity. Volleyball, soccer, wrestling, fireworks, parades, music, and dancing are some of the things which go into making up this great carnival-like affair throughout Afghanistan.

JEWS see ETHNIC GROUPS

JINN. Evil spirits, which according to the Afghan lore, possess a person and cause sickness. Usual symptoms of such possession are loss of balance, incoherent speech, sweating and general anxiety. Religious specialists, by performing specific rituals, may relieve a person of such possessions. The Jinn are active at night and in the dark; thus, being alone in a dark area should be avoided. It is believed that when in company, the Jinn will not attempt to possess a person. As a rule, Jinn are perhaps best understood for explaining and controlling any individual's deviation in behavior, physical, emotional, or psychological.

JIRGAH see LOYA JIRGAH

JOZJAN (PROVINCE). A province located in north central Afghanistan whose capital is Sheberghan. It ranks 11th in size among the provinces of the country. It extends from the Amu Darya in the north to the Hindu Kush in the south. Natural gas fields, which have been discovered in the province, are an important part of the economy as are the Qaraqul sheep herds. Sheberghan (q.v.) and Aqcha (q.v.) in the north are centers for the distribution of the carpets woven by the people here. Buzkashi (see GAMES AND SPORTS) is a popular sport in all parts of the province.

JUM'A. Friday. The holiday of the week in both the solar and lunar calendars of Afghanistan. On this day almost all the business shops (with few exceptions, such as bakeries and pharmacies), government offices and schools are closed.

JURISPRUDENCE see HANAFI

JUY. The water streams running along the main thoroughfares in large Afghan towns and in the cities. The functions for which the Juy water is used depend largely upon the quality of its water.

-K-

KABAB. Roasted meat which is very popular in the home, restaurants, and tea shops.

KABUL (CITY). Capital of the province of Kabul and capital of the nation, this city has been in existence for over 3,300 years. The Rig Veda (compiled between 1400 and 900 B.C.) refers to this city by the name of Kubha. Kabura is the name used by Ptolemy in the 2nd century B.C. The location of the city has changed several times. Before the time of Christ, it appears to have been located on the southern slopes of the Hindu Kush. During the Graeco-Bactrian age it was located in the plains of Bagram. Later it was located behind the Sherdarwaza mountain and the small hill on which the citadel is located.

The city was destroyed once by Alauddin Jahansooz and later by the British. The Arabs, over a period of some 200 years, attacked the city and were repulsed. The city was destroyed and rebuilt many times during this period. Two centuries ago an earthquake leveled the city. The city, with high mountains on each side, at the time of the Arab invasion in the 7th century A.D. was accessible only by means of the narrow Guzargah Pass. From 1504 to 1738 it was part of the Mongul Empire. During the first and second Afghan Wars, a great deal of fighting took place here when it was occupied by the British in 1839-42 and in 1879-80. Under Abdul Rahman Khan, the ruling monarch beginning in 1880, modern development of the city began. It presently centers in the suburbs of Sherpur and Naway Kabul (new Kabul), to the north and west. There are many modern buildings as well as a modern airport. The country's trade with the east is controlled from Kabul and there has been an increase in industrial development in recent years. Wool and cotton textiles, leather goods, canned and processed fruit and foods, cement, automobile parts, and military equipment and weapons are produced

Kabul (Province) 68

in factories receiving hydroelectric power from a
station at Sarobi. Archaeological remains are
numerous within and around the city.

KABUL (PROVINCE). A province in southeast Afghanistan. With an area of about 11,000 square miles, Kabul ranks 28th in size among the provinces. Its capital, Kabul City, is also the capital of the country. The Chardehi district is very picturesque and very fertile. Food for the city of Kabul is produced here by the many skilled farmers and fruit raisers. Kabul's airport is located in the Deh Sabz district, also a very fertile area. Kabul's new industrial district is also found here. The districts of Kalai Murad Big, Sarai Khwaja, and Karabagh are among the best grape-growing areas of the country. Paghman district, 25 km. from Kabul and 900 meters higher, is a valley in the Kohe Baba Range. It is a pleasant retreat for many from the heat of the summer and thousands vacation there each summer. There is little tillable land around Paghman and many of the people commute to Kabul City to work.

KABUL BASIN. The Kabul River and its tributaries flow into the Kabul Basin. The most important tributaries are the Logar, the Panjsher, the Tagab, the Alishing, the Alingar and the Kunar. Although some of these dry up in the summer, they are all widely used for irrigation when possible.
    The catchment area in the Kabul is approximately 30,000 square miles. See also RIVERS.

KABUL MUSEUM. Located in Dar ul Aman (q.v.), this is the largest museum in Afghanistan. It houses specimens from all the historic and prehistoric archaeological sites in Afghanistan. The museum also has extensive ethnographic displays depicting the variety of ethnic and cultural traditions in Afghanistan. The Afghan Institute of Archaeology supervises the museum.

KABUL RIVER. This river rises in the Unai pass in
the Kohe Baba and extends for about 250 miles
(150 of it in Afghanistan) before it joins the Indua.
It is the most important river in eastern Afghanistan.
During the summer, there is only a small
amount of water running at Kabul City. Between
Kabul and Jalalabad, however, the waters are
held back by three dams. The river is navigable
below Jalalabad. Its tributaries are crucial to
the productivity of much of the land in the country.
For tributaries see KABUL BASIN. See also
RIVERS.

KABUL RIVER VALLEY. A very fertile valley with a
sub-tropical climate, it is one of the major agricultural
areas of the country. It lies around the
city of Jalalabad and is densely populated. Its
location on a trade route across the Khyber Pass
increases its economic value. Its climate is particularly
suited for fruit growing.

KABUL TIMES. An English daily newspaper published
in Kabul. It is published on a regular basis, and
provides an adequate account of national and international
news.

KABUL UNIVERSITY. Established in the carly 1930's,
it is the oldest institution of higher learning in
Afghanistan. It began with a faculty of medicine,
and at the present time has faculties of law, economics,
agriculture, science, literature, theology,
education and engineering. The university is totally
subsidized by the state, and is administratively
under the jurisdiction of the national ministry
of education. Kabul University became a
coeducational institution in the late 1950s.

KAFIRISTAN see NURISTAN (AREA)

KAJAKI POWER PLANT see HELMAND VALLEY

KAJULA KADPHISE I (15-78 A. D.). Chief of the
Kushans who imposed his authority on the rest

of the Yüeh-chi tribes and united the Yüeh-chi into a powerful military machine. He is said to have taken over at about 40 A.D. Along with his control over the north, he attempted to control the provinces to the south of the Hindu Kush as well. He was successful in taking Ki-Pan (Capisa), Kao-fu (Kabul), Pouta (Zabulistan), and Gardez. His area of control extended from Sogdonia to the Indus and perhaps to the Jhelum.

He was succeeded by his son Vima Kadphises (Kadphises II) (q.v.)

KAKAR, M. HASAN. A young contemporary Afghan (Pushtun) historian, who has written extensively about the history of Afghanistan. Kakar is a new breed of Afghan scholar who uses original Afghan sources in his work and does not paraphrase non-Afghan renditions of the history of Afghanistan. His works on the period during the following Amir Abdul Rahman Khan's reign (1880-1901) are of particular importance.

KANDAHAR see QANDAHAR

KANISHKA THE GREAT. Ascended the throne ca. 144 A.D. and was an outstanding soldier, statesman, and administrator. Under him, Gandhara became an important cultural center--literature and the arts as well as religion grew to great heights. During his rule the Kushan empire reached its pinnacle. His armies extended their boundaries in all directions. A victory in the east took Kashmir, Sinkiang, Kashgar, Yarkand, Khotan, and all the Chinese provinces north of Tibet and east of the Pamirs and freed them from the forced tribute they were paying to China. Kanishka's capital was in Purshapur (Peshawar), and his summer capital was Capisa (Bagram today). At one time Kanishka was a follower of Zoroastrianism and later became a Buddhist and convened the Fourth Council of the Buddhist monks during his reign. At this meeting, which brought together over five hundred monks from all over the

Kapisa (Province)

Buddhist world, the foundation of the new school--Mahayana (q.v.) ("the Great Wheel") was laid.

Kanishka was also a builder. He directed the building of great monuments and monasteries, especially in his capitals. At his winter capital he is said to have erected a <u>sangharama</u> (a major temple) with a stupa perhaps 45 meters high--probably one of the most beautiful and impressive temples at that time.

He also encouraged many in the fields of literature, art, and science. Commerce increased and contacts with foreign peoples brought new life to all of his endeavors. The country was in a key position along trade routes between China and the Mediterranean and from Turkestan through the Hindu Kush to the Indian subcontinent. This period came to a close in the 3rd century when the Kushans were out of power. See also HISTORY--Buddhist Period.

KAPISA (PROVINCE). A province located in east central Afghanistan. With an area of 4,658 sq. km., Kapisa ranks 26th in size in the country. Its capital is Mahmood Ragi and its governor (1970) is Nasratullah Malekyar. Rivers in the province include the Nejrab, the Tagab, the Panjsher, the latter being a popular fishing spot. Another popular attraction for vacationers is the "running sands" of Rezakohistan. Different dunes are formed during the day and these, together with an ancient cave, attract many people. Farm products include mulberries, pomegranates, wheat, barley and other grains. A popular product of the Panjsher district is talkhan--a rich sweet made with mulberries and nuts. The Nejrab district is well-known for its cheeses. Pomegranates are the chief product of the Tagab district. The largest textile plant in the country, the Gulbahar Mills (1970 annual production capacity of 80,000 meters) is located in this province of Kapisa.

KARAKUL see QARAQUL

KAREZ see QANAT

KAWGAN RIVER see HERAT BASIN

KELAY. A pushtu term usually meaning a small village, community, or hamlet. See also QARYAH.

KHASH RUD RIVER. This river rises in the Siah Koh Mountains about 130 miles northwest of Kandahar, and follows a 250-mile southwesterly course. Around the towns of Dilarum, Khash, and Chakhansur it waters oases and then flows to the Seistan lacustrine depression of the west, where it empties into the Seistan Lake. See also SEISTAN BASIN and RIVERS.

KHAYL. The Pushtu term for a lineage.

KHAYR KHANA. An archaeological site located about seven miles from Kabul in a pass separating the Kabul Valley from Kohistan. It is one of the several sites providing evidence for the fusion of Kushan, Sassanian, and Hindu art styles and motifs.

KHERQA. A cloak allegedly worn by Prophet Mohammed. One of these cloaks was presented to Ahmad Shah Durrani by the Amir of Bukhara, Murad Beg. Ahmad Shah built a mosque in Qandahar specifically designed to house the Kherqa. Both are still preserved and intact. As any item attributed to the Prophet of Islam, the Kherqa and the encompassing mosque are frequently visited by Muslims in Afghanistan particularly on the occasion of Muslim Holidays.

KHILAPHATE. The succession of leaders following the Prophet Mohammed. The first four of the successors are called khulapha-i-Rashidin in Arabic. Abu Bakr, Omar, Osman, and Ali respectively followed Prophet Mohammed. At the time of the Prophet's death, it was argued that Ali, a member of his patriline and his son-in-law, should succeed him (consistent with the patrilineal and patrifocal descent pattern operative at the time of the Prophet). But this did not happen. Abu Bakr, the Prophet's father-in-law, succeeded him as the first Khalipha. Thus the seeds for major divisions in Islam were sown. Later, after the death of the third Khalif, Osman, some Muslims argued that Ali should have been the first successor to Prophet Mohammed. Until today the major divisive factor between the two major sects of Islam, sunni and shi'a, remains unresolved. The sunni sect agrees with the order of succession as it happened. The shi'a sect argues that the legitimate successor of Prophet Mohammed was and should have been Ali, since he was in the Prophet's patrilineage and Abu Bakr was not.

KHULM RIVER. Rises in the northern foothills of the Hindu Kush and follows a 130-mile course north to the Kara-Kum desert of Turkmenistan in the Soviet Union. See also RIVERS.

KHUSHHAL KHAN KHATAK (1613-1690). One of the great 17th-century Pushtun poets. During his lifetime he was the chief of his Pushtun tribe (Khatak). His poems epitomize the Pushtun warrior-poet, a combination of personality dimensions idealized throughout the Afghan cultures. He constantly found beauty in nature and in man. He was, in addition to being a poet, a great and perceptive political leader who led military missions against the Moghuls of India in defense of freedom for the Pushtuns, and recognized the destructiveness of the Pushtun intra- and inter-tribal conflicts. He is one of the very few Pushtun literary-historical leaders whose work has been seriously noticed in the West.

KHWAJA ABDULLAH ANSARI. Patron saint of the city of Herat, he was a great exponent of Islamic thought. He is the son of Abu Mansoor Mohammed who was a well-known scholar. His "title" was "Pir-i-Herat" (Saint of Herat). He studied at the

Milini School of Herat, and is said to have been
a most serious scholar. He is one of the best
known Sufi poets of this time. He authored the
Diwan, in Arabic, which contains more than
6,000 couplets. His Persian verses have been
estimated at 14,000--devoted to Divine Lore. He
is known as well for his Manajat (Invocations)
which have been translated into many languages
including English.

KHWAJA AMRAN MOUNTAIN RANGE. Runs southwestward between the Qandahar region and the Pakistan frontier. See also GEOGRAPHY.

KHYBER PASS. A historic mountain pass situated in
the middle of the area where Pushtun tribes have
been historically and are presently situated. The
Khyber Pass is located close to the eastern boundary of Afghanistan, and is one of the points
through which one can enter Afghanistan by land.
The pass has been an important point in the routes
of the invading armies which came from Greece,
Central Asia, and Afghanistan to conquer and rule
the Indian subcontinent. The Khyber Pass crosses
the Safid Koh Mountain Range, and links the Kabul
River Valley to Peshawar at about 3,500 feet.
The 28-mile Khyber gorge has been of political
and military importance since prehistoric times.

KHYRAT. Large amounts of food which can be given
to the poor during the ceremonies and parties at
the various post-burial ceremonies. A khyrat
can also be given when a wish or hope has been
fulfilled.

KING MOHAMMAD NADIR SHAH. King of Afghanistan
from 1929-1933. Born in 1880, he was a member
of the family of the Mohammedzai dynasty which
reigned in Afghanistan until 1973. Prior to becoming king, he served as the commander and
chief of the Afghan forces and later as Minister
of War. In 1924 he became Minister Plenipotentiary

of Afghanistan in Paris. His son, Mohammad Zahir, studied in France during this time. A civil war broke out in Afghanistan in 1929 and Mohammad Nadir Shah returned to Afghanistan. When peace was restored in October, 1929, Mohammad Nadir Shah was selected King. He reigned until November 8, 1933, when he was assassinated and his son, Mohammad Zahir, was brought to the throne.

KING MOHAMMAD ZAHIR. Born in Kabul on October 15, 1914. He attended school in Afghanistan from 1920 to 1924. In that year his father, Mohammad Nadir Shah, was appointed as the Minister Plenipotentiary of Afghanistan to Paris and Mohammad Zahir accompanied him. He went to various schools in France until 1930 when, following a civil war, his father was selected King and he returned to Afghanistan. Mohammad Zahir then entered the Royal Afghanistan Infantry School in Kabul. In September of 1933 he became Acting Minister of Education. In November of that year, his father was assassinated and Mohammad Zahir was brought to the throne. Universal education for all, among other accomplishments, has been among the plans and programs supported by this former King. A series of Five-Year Plans, begun in 1956 (then under the leadership of Premier Daud), has organized the development and implementation of many projects such as roads, power plants, factories, etc. A new constitution was written in 1964. The 1964 constitution was partially revoked by the Republican Regime after the revolution of July 17, 1973.

KIRGHIZ see ETHNIC GROUPS

KIRGHIZI see LANGUAGES

KOHE BABA MOUNTAIN RANGE. Located in central Afghanistan, it is separated from the Hindu Kush by the Bamyan Valley. It runs westward for about 125 miles. Its highest peak is Shah Fuladi

(16,872 feet). Several other peaks rise to about 15,000 feet. See also GEOGRAPHY.

KOHZAD, AHMAD ALI. A prominent contemporary Afghan historian, known primarily for a definitive historic work which he completed during the late 1960s. See also Bibliography.

KOKCHA RIVER. This river rises in northern Hindu Kush west of Chitral. Along its 200-mile flow, it provides the necessary water for several important agricultural areas, especially near Zebak and Faizabad. It is the major river of the northeast part of the country and is a tributary of the Amu Darya River. See also AMU DARYA RIVER and RIVERS.

KOLA. A small head cap worn with a turban. See also CLOTHING.

KORAN see QUR'AN

KORRUKH RIVER see HERAT BASIN and RIVERS

KUBHA see KABUL

KUCHIS. The pastoral nomads of Afghanistan, these ethnic groups comprise a significant proportion of the population of the country. They usually migrate annually to the green valleys north and south of the Hindu Kush. They coexist in a symbiotic pattern with the sedentary socio-cultural groupings along their migration paths. Recent Afghan Government plans have encouraged the nomads to settle newly irrigated areas in southwestern Afghanistan. The Kuchis in Afghanistan belong primarily to the Gilzai tribes of the Pushtuns. In parts of Afghanistan they are called pawindas.

KUNAR (PROVINCE). A province located in the southeastern part of the country. Its capital is Asadabad. It ranks sixth among the provinces of Afghanistan in terms of size. Rice and sugar

cane are the most important products of the province, though the climate and abundance of water also make it a good area for raisins, apples, pears, grapes, oranges, mulberries, lemons, and walnuts. Hunting birds with ropes and nets is a popular pastime of many Kunar men.
    There is a great celebration in Asadabad during Jeshn (Celebration of Independence). People come from miles around to take part in the carnival-like festivities.

KUNAR RIVER. Rising in northeastern Hindu Kush, this river follows a 250-mile course southwest to join the Kabul River at Jalalabad. It is important to the transportation of timber and irrigation.

KUNDUZ see QUNDUZ

KUSHANS see BAMYAN (PROVINCE) and HISTORY-- Buddhist Period

-L-

LAGHMAN (PROVINCE). Located in the east-central part of Afghanistan, its capital is Miterlam and it ranks 23rd in area among the provinces. Rice and wheat are the province's most important crops. Varieties of rice grown include pashayee, deradooni, and bara. Most of it is grown in the Valleys of Alinger and Absling. The Valley of Nuristan, located in this province, is the home of the people who are well-known for their wood carving. See also NURISTAN.

LALMEE. Nonirrigated farming in areas of Afghanistan where water for irrigation and irrigation technology are nonexistent. Lalmee also refers to dry farmed land. Cultivated land under this mode of agriculture is solely dependent on rain water.

LANDY. Dried meat which is quite common in the winter diet of Afghans. See also FOOD.

LANGUAGES. The major languages spoken in Afghanistan are: Pushtu, Dari (Afghan Persian), Farsi, Nuristani, Moghuli, Uzbeki, Turkmani, Tajiki, and Kirghizi. Overall, about twenty languages or dialects are spoken in the country. However, almost all Afghans are bilingual, and four-fifths of the population speak either Dari or Pushtu--both variants of the Indo-European language family. Pushtu, the indigenous language of the largest tribal group, is spoken, primarily, through southern and eastern Afghanistan and has been declared the national language of the country. Nevertheless, Dari has always predominated in the cities and remains the official language in the administration, government, and bureaucracies. In spite of the fact that most Afghans can speak at least two languages, only about 15 per cent of the total population can read and write. See also ETHNIC GROUPS.

LAPIS LAZULI. Afghanistan is rich in lapis lazuli, one of the preferred gems throughout Central and Southwest Asia. It has been mined for more than 4,000 years in the province of Badakhshan. Important quantities of lapis lazuli have also been found in the Pamir knot. Most lapis lazuli is obtained from government-owned mines and is cut and finished at the lapidarium in Kabul. Production of lapis lazuli has risen in the past few years, and much of it is exported.

LASHKAR GAH. The newest model town in Afghanistan. It is the capital of Helmand Province. The town is built around the Helmand Arghandab Valley Authority (HAVA). New residential and government buildings and a modern hotel have recently been built. Historical sites of the ruins of the Ghaznavi Dynasty are located in the old Lashkar Gah (also called Lashkari Bazaar) on the banks of the Helmand River. Archaeologists have uncovered the remains of the splendors of the Ghaznavid Period, including palaces, courtyards, archways at the entrances to the city, military barracks, the old city, and rich and exquisite bazaars. The town is located about 85 miles west of Qandahar.

LASHKARI BAZAAR see LASHKAR GAH

LEVIRATE. A practice, common in parts of Afghanistan, requiring or permitting a man to marry the widow of his brother or other very close male kin. The offspring of a levirate marriage are sometimes considered to be descendants of the deceased brother of the close kin. The primary logic for this practice is to keep a widow in her deceased husband's group. Since the acquisition of a wife is foremost a socio-economic investment, the existence of the levirate mechanism will insure that the woman will stay with her husband's group when and if the husband dies.

LITERATURE. Poetry is generally considered the highest form of literary expression. Not only are most of the Afghan scholars poets, but each ethnic group and each village community has its own epics, short verses, and songs. Such folklore, as well as poems by well-known poets of the past, have found their way into the lives of the people, transmitted orally from generation to generation by professional minstrels who move about the country entertaining villagers at tea houses and by nomadic travellers at major stopping points (called caravansarais). Much of this body of literature has only recently been recorded.

Epics and short verses, regardless of ethnic source, show considerable similarity. The most popular themes are war, love, jealousy, respect for age, filial piety, acceptance of parental authority, the joys of having children, riches and happiness, and religious-Islamic folklore. All are more or less tinctured with Islamic sentiment, and many are intended to instill courage and traditional virtues of Afghan society.

Much of the contemporary prose and poetry written in Dari and Pushtu utilizes the heroic, religious-mystical, or lyric themes of classical

Persian and Pushtu literature.
    Elements of social criticism have appeared in the poems and prose of contemporary Pushtu and Dari authors. Conservatism and the traditional social structure of the Afghan society are frequently criticized in the works of present day Afghan authors.

LMOONZ. A Pushtu word for prayer. See also NIMAZ.

LOGAR (PROVINCE). A province located in southeast Afghanistan. Its capital is Pule Alam and it ranks 27th in area among the provinces. Logar is well-known for its distinctive dance music and its musicians travel to many parts of the country to perform. The tobacco raised in the province is well-known for its good taste. Important crops are barley, fruit, rice, and wheat, and much of this is sent to Kabul. An intricate canal system aids in the growing of crops and, because of this, many areas are able to raise two crops a year. The district of Charkh is known for its apricots, mulberries, and peaches. Shutur Gardan, Do Bandi, and Patkhab Shana are important producers of cherries, prunes, and walnuts. Almonds are also grown and are found on Kohsar Mountain. The capital of Logar province is Baraki Barak.

LOGAR RIVER. Rising in the southwest extension of the Hindu Kush, this river follows a 150-mile course and joins with the Kabul River just east of Kabul and flows into the Kabul Basin. This river is known in its central section as the Wardak River. See also RIVERS.

LOY WOLOSWAL. The administrator or commissioner of a major administrative district within a province.

LOYA JIRGAH. National council of notables, tribal chiefs, religious leaders, which may be called to assembly when a major issue, problem, or reform is considered to be facing the nation. It is based on the Pushtun institution of jirgah, which in tribal organization refers to the council of elders, tribal leaders, lineages, clans, or the heads of families. The traditional functions of the jirgah are resolution of inter- and intra-tribal conflicts and disputes about land ownership, blood vengeance, and sometimes the organization of war against outsiders.

LOYA WOLOSWALI. A major administrative district within an Afghan province.

LUNGI see DASTAR

-M-

MAHAYANA BUDDHISM. The foundations of this school of thought were laid at the Fourth Council of the Buddhist Monks, called by Kanishka the Great (ca. 2nd century). Mahayana means, literally, "the Great Wheel." This is in contrast to Hinayana or "Smaller Wheel." At this point, under the new principles of the faith, the founder of Buddhism was deified and this image became an object of religious worship. This Northern School was influenced by Hellenism and underwent many changes from the original Southern School or Hinayana, and developed into a new religion.

MAHMOOD RAQI. Capital of Kapisa Province. Mahmood Raqi is a small agricultural town, located on the Ghor Band River. It is located about 25 miles north of Kabul.

MAHMOOD'S TOMB. Located near Ghazni, Mahmood's tomb and two magnificent towers of victory erected by Mahmood upon his triumphant return from the conquest of the Punjab in India in 1026 are all that remain of a great center built during his reign. The rest of the city was burned by Alauddin, "the World Burner," who not only burned the city, but purportedly led a rampage on the populace which killed 70,000 people in seven days.

MAIDAN. Capital of Wardak Province. Located about 20 miles west of Kabul, Maidan Shahr (formerly Maidan or Kote Ashrao) is a small town situated on the Julga River. In addition to being the administrative center of the Wardak Province, it serves as a market place for the surrounding agricultural communities.

MAIMANA. Capital of Fariab Province. Located about 280 miles northeast of Herat, Maimana is accessible by automobile and air. The town is the largest commercial center of this province which is famous for horse breeding and Qaraqul sheep (q.v.). Maimana in historic times served as the political center for local tribal chiefdoms. It has a large bazaar, good hotels, and elaborate chaikhanas (q.v.).

MAIWAND. A battlefield, west of Qandahar, where the British military troops were decisively defeated by the Afghan Army led by Mohammed Ayub Khan on July 27, 1880. This is referred to in literature as the famous Battle of Maiwand. See also ANGLO-AFGHAN WARS.

MALIK. The usual term for a selected local chief of a village or small community. The village chief, chosen by the villagers, is the main channel of communication between them and the provincial and central government. Where the entire population of a village belongs to one clan or lineage, the position of chief tends to be the hereditary privilege of the senior member of the lineage. Usually the oldest son inherits the office. Sometimes the Maliks represent the interests of absentee landlords. They are instrumental in resolving conflicts on local levels. In predominantly Turkman and Uzbek areas, the equivalent status to Malik is called Arbab.

MALIKI see HANAFI

MANAJAT   see   KHWAJA ABDULLAH ANSARI

MANDEEL   see   DASTAR

MANQAL   see   SANDALI

MANUCHEHRI.   A poet during the Ghaznavid period.

MASJID.   The Afghan native term for the Mosque.
Every Afghan village, town, and city has an adequate number of Masjids to serve its population. A Mullah is usually the caretaker of the Masjid. Daily collective and Friday noon prayers are performed in the Masjid. In remote areas the Masjid serves as a rooming house for travellers. Funeral services are performed in the Masjid and important community meetings also take place here.

MASJIDE JAME or FRIDAY MOSQUE.   A center for mystics and scholars located in Herat. Much lavish work was performed on the building by calligraphers and tilemakers. The great Sufi poet and philosopher Khwaja Abdullah Ansari (q.v.) taught here in the 11th century.

MAULANA JALALUDDIN RUMI (MANLANA HALAND DIN BALKHI).   Author of the Mathnawi, a great piece of literature. He was a protégé of Hakeem Sanai and became himself one of the three top mystic poets of Persian literature. He emigrated to Turkey (Konia) and died there around 1273. See also HAKEEM SANAI.

MAYRMANA.   An honorific title (in Pushtu) referring to a woman who is married. It is comparable to "Mrs.," "Lady," or "Madam."

MAZARE SHARIF.   Capital of Balkh Province, it is located about 270 miles north-northwest of Kabul. The city is a busy commercial center as well as a major depot and transportation point for qaraqul pelts and agricultural products. Mazare Sharif

is fast becoming an important industrial city as
a thermal power station, fertilizer, textile, and
raisin factories, and modern tanneries develop.
The city houses a new textile plant which reportedly
produces ten to fifteen million meters of cloth
annually. Rising in the center of the city is the
impressive shrine of Hazrat-i-Ali, son-in-law and
cousin of the Prophet Mohammed. It is alleged
that Ali is buried at this shrine. Other cities in
Iran and in Iraq make similar claims. The city
is visited by countless pilgrims and tourists
throughout the year and particularly on the Afghan
(solar) New Year's Day. The "Festival of Tulips"
is held during the first days of the Afghan new
year. Mazare Sharif has a museum and expansive
bazaars, hotels, and restaurants. Regular air
service is available to the city from Kabul.

MECCA   see   ISLAM

MEDINA   see   ISLAM

MELMASTIA. To entertain guests and to feed and
shelter them in accordance with the obligation of
Melmastia is a matter of prestige. Among some
Pushtuns, it is normally the duty of the individual
household; among others, each village and town
maintains a guesthouse at which travelers and
callers are entertained. The ability to entertain
is a culturally approved manner of displaying
wealth, winning political allegiances, and a tribal
chief's standing is often measured by his manner
of entertaining guests. They may seldom be
turned out or away, but they are expected to stay
no longer than three days. Hospitality extended
to kinsmen is taken for granted and does not
count as hospitality. It must be extended to
known enemies as lavishly as to friends or
strangers. In turn the guest--no matter what
reason he has to suspect that his host or their
fellow villagers are hostile to him--is expected
to behave in an entirely friendly manner as long
as he is a guest. The guest house in Pushtu is
called Hujra.

MINERALS. Afghanistan is known to possess deposits of chrome, copper, lead, zinc, uranium, manganese, asbestos, gold, silver, iron, sulfur, mica, nickel, slate, salt, and lapis lazuli. Amethyst, beryl, ruby, alabaster, tourmaline, jade, and quartz-bearing rocks also occur. Granite, white and colored marble, porphyry, gypsum, fire clay, limestone, china clay, talc, and soapstone are found in significant quantities. Such pigments as cinnabar, and red and yellow ocher can be easily mined. Outcroppings of coal and seepages of oil and pitch occur both north and south of the Hindu Kush Mountains.

Promising layers of oil bearing shales were found in the north during an exploratory survey, and additional deposits were discovered later in the Arghandab Valley. Natural gas deposits have been found and produced in Jozjan Province. Of Afghanistan's other mineral resources, only coal, salt, and lapis lazuli have been exploited to any significant extent.

MINHAJ EIRAJ. An important citizen of the province of Jozjan during the 13th century. He left Jozjan during the Mongol invasions for the Court of Delhi in India where he became a notable administrator, jurist, and scholar. Here he wrote his History of the Ghaznavids, Ghorids, and Early Muslim Kings of India.

MIR WAIS HOTAK. A Pushtun chieftain who declared Qandahar independent from Persian rule in 1709 A.D. He ruled for about six years and established the Ghilzai Dynasty of rulers in Afghanistan and in Iran. His mausoleum is located about five miles west of Qandahar. See also GHILZAI DYNASTY and GHILZAI TRIBES.

MIR-AB. A man in most Afghan villages and farming communities who allocates the water, chooses the time for the annual repair of ditches and qanats, and sees to it that all participating farming families do their proper share of the upkeep. In the Hazarajat, where the population is sparse and irrigation water is not abundant, the Mir-Ab's position does not exist.

MITERLAM. A new town, now the capital of the province of Laghman in east-central Afghanistan. The town was named after a holy man whose shrine is located there. Miterlam is an agricultural and commercial market place.

MOGHUL   see   ETHNIC GROUPS

MOGHUL DYNASTY   see   TIMURE LUNG

MOGHULI   see   LANGUAGES

MOHAMMED AYUB KHAN   see   MAIWAND and ANGLO-AFGHAN WARS

MOHAMMEDZAI DYNASTY   see   DURRANI DYNASTIES

MONARCHS   see   DURRANI DYNASTIES

MORGENSTIERNE, GEORG. A Scandinavian scholar who has done much original research on the languages of Afghanistan. His publications, especially on Pushtu, Dari, and Nuristani, are of particular basic importance. See also Bibliography.

MOSQUE   see   MASJID

MOUNTAINS   see   GEOGRAPHY

MUA'ZIN. The person who announces, in Arabic, the call for daily prayer from the minaret of a mosque. The Mua'zin are respected members of their communities throughout Afghanistan. See also AZAN.

MULLAH. Throughout Afghanistan the Mullahs are religious leaders. They are also influential in education and politics. Generally, they are a most important and influential group in the country and have a great deal of religious prestige. The

Mullahs are conservative and generally opposed to
progressive socio-cultural change. Their influence
is greatest in non-urban areas. Functionally, they
are the caretakers of local Masjids (Mosques) and
are active in the affairs of the communities in
which they reside.

MULLAH NASRUDDIN. A comic figure and trickster
purveying fun and jokes throughout Afghanistan and
the Muslim world. In the Afghan lore, he is por-
trayed as a sharp operator who outwits all his op-
ponents. Often he becomes trapped in his own
net of intrigues, and at other times he attacks
traditional dicta and society to make a moral point.

MUNDIGAK. An archaeological site dating from the
Bronze Age, it is located in the province of
Kandahar, twelve miles from the capital. It appears that between 3000 and 1000 B.C. this was
a crossroads for those traveling from the Indus
Valley, Iran, and Mesopotamia.
    Work done by Louis Dupree at the site in-
dicates that the prehistoric occupations covered an
area of about 20 hectares. Findings here include
alabaster vessels, flint artifacts, terra cotta figures and stone seals. Elaborate pottery styles
were found as well as a palace and a temple.
See also DEH MORASI GHONDAI.

MURGHAB RIVER. One of the major rivers of the
northwest basin. It rises in the Koh-i-Baba,
flows westward about 350 miles and turns north
to the Kara-Kum desert of Turkmanistan in the
Soviet Union. See also RIVERS.

MUSIC. Afghans appreciate music and enjoy singing.
In the cities there are public performances of
both singing and dancing by professionals. The
professional troups often travel through the
country. Although professional, indigenous musicians are not held in high social esteem, amateur
performers carry no stigma. Many young men
and boys play instruments, usually drums or

stringed instruments. In the countryside the people sing mostly without accompaniment. Afghan music, by and large differs from Western music in scales, note intervals, pitch and rhythm, but nonetheless, has a greater resemblance to it than is usually found in Asian music. Orchestras include a number of stringed instruments, drums and a handpumped harmonium (harmonia). See also MUSICAL INSTRUMENTS.

MUSICAL INSTRUMENTS. The most popular and widely indigenous musical instruments in Afghanistan are:
Dhol: A two-headed membranophone. The heads are made of animal skin and are retained and tightened by means of continuous loops of a single twisted cord passing through both heads at several points. The dhol is suspended from the neck of the musician and played with hands or sticks.
Dholak: A pair of single-headed kettle drums. The drums are played with drumsticks, traditionally made out of walnut. They are popular in the Ghazni area.
Daira: A single-headed membranophone found throughout Afghanistan. It is usually played in a vertical position with the rim resting on the extended palm of one hand while beaten with the fingers of the other hand.
Zerbaghali: Single-headed membranophone. The body is made of baked clay and has several concentric designs. The head is made out of goatskin. When played, it is held under one arm and is beaten with both hands.
Tambur: Metal strings passing over a bridge (usually of ivory) which rests on the wooden face of the resonating chamber (made of a gourd). It is played throughout Afghanistan.
Rubab: The face of this Tambur-like stringed instrument is made of goatskin and the body out of wood.
Dhambura: A very common string instrument in Afghanistan. The dhambura is a crude sitar-like instrument with two or three strings.
Ghichak: A bowed chordophone. The two strings,

cylindrical neck, and carved peg-head comprise the total instrument. The resonating box is a round frame of wood covered with goatskin. It is played in a vertical position with a bow.
Sarani: Another variety of a bowed chordophone, found primarily in Nuristan.
Tula: A flipped-mouthed whistle flute.
Surnai: A variation on the flute with a conical bore at the out end. There are seven fingerholes on the frontal plane and one thumbhole on the dorsal plane.

MUSULMAN. Another term for a Muslim. Literally, it means a "Muslim-Person."

MUQUR. A town southwest of Ghazni. It is a major stopping point between Qandahar and Ghazni. Close by is a large salt lake, the largest in Afghanistan.

MUTUFER see CHENGIS KHAN

-N-

NAALI. Wooden clogs worn by many Afghan countrymen and women.

NAHOOR RIVER see GHAZNI BASIN

NAIZA BAZI. A very exciting sport of "tent pegging" played in the province of Zabul. Riders race at full speed down a large field and try to spear pegs which are planted 20 cms. deep into the ground. It takes a very skilled rider and a well-trained horse to play this game well. Some players are beginning to take the sport to audiences in Kabul.

NAN. One of the main staples of the Afghan diet. It is made of unleavened whole wheat or barley. It is formed into large, flat cakes and baked in earthen ovens, called tandur in Dari, tanoor in Pushtu. The Pushtu term for this kind of bread is dodai.

NANAWATI. This is a special form of hospitality and a palliative to the harsh concepts of badal (q.v.). An individual pursued by his enemies, or otherwise in apprehension for his life, can seek asylum with other Pushtuns, who are then required to protect him as if they had kinship ties with him (which would make such protection mandatory). Asylum can be sought in the village mosque, shrine, or in the home of any tribesman. Breaches in nanawati, refusal to extend it, or breach of its rules by either protector or pursuer, are serious infractions of pushtunwali.

NANGARHAR (PROVINCE). A province located in southeast Afghanistan. Its capital is Jalalabad and it ranks 25th in size among Afghan provinces. This ancient area is second only to Kabul in population density. It has long been an important cultural center with emphasis on food producing. Thousands of pieces of sculpture dating back at least from the 2nd to the 6th centuries A.D. have been found at a site just south of Jalalabad (q.v.). During these early times this was a spot to which Buddhist pilgrims came. Most of the sculpture is now housed in the Hadda Rooms of the Kabul Museum (q.v.) or in the Musée Guiment d'Art Asiatiques in Paris.
    Thousands of visitors now come to the area to enjoy the sun on their holidays. In 1963 the Nangarhar Medical School was established. Its main objective is preventive medicine with Health Education as its major focus. See also DARUNTA DAM.

NASER KHOSRAU. A philosopher-poet who lived during the Ghaznavid period. He was a powerful interpreter, and wrote many poems and didactic treaties.

NAWROZ. The first day of the Afghan solar year, it is celebrated as the New Year in Afghanistan. Nawroz falls on about March 21, and it is a one-day national holiday. Much dried fruit (softened

by being soaked in water) is consumed. Friends
and relatives visit each other. Public tree-plant-
ing ceremonies are performed in towns and cities.
The holiday falls on the first day of Hamal, the
first month of the Afghan solar year.

NEOLITHIC. The "New Stone Age." The period from
3,500 to 7,500 years before historical times. It
is also called the "Late Stone Age." Weaving,
pottery, fine flint working, the bow and arrow,
and many metal tools are characteristic of this
period, as are the wheel, a primitive pastoralism
and agriculture, and a lack of ferrous and bronze
metallurgy. A major characteristic of the Neolithic
is an economy which is self-sufficient in food production. The period is also marked by a shift
from chipped to polished stone tools. Rice, maize,
barley, wheat, and other cereals domesticated then
are still present today.
   The Neolithic in Afghanistan has been divided into two phases:
1. Non-Ceramic Neolithic: Domesticated sheep
and goats have been identified at the archaeological
site Aq Kupruk I. There are also plant remains
which were probably domesticated. Among these
plants are wheat and barley. Evidence for the
domestication of sheep and goats exists. A date
of 20,000 years is tentatively given for the domestication of wheat. If this proves to be correct,
the Neolithic of Afghanistan will have to be considered one of the earliest.
2. Ceramic Neolithic: At the Aq Kupruk I and II
levels evidence exists for the introduction at this
later phase of the Neolithic of pottery, limestone
hoes, manos, metates, polishers, celts, and many
chert tools including cores, sickle blades, micro-
points, and drills. The faunal remains of the
phase of Neolithic include domesticated sheep,
goats, and cattle.

NIMAZ. A Dari word meaning "prayer." The word is
indigenous to the Iranian Plateau and is commonly
used to mean both prayer and prayer-time in

Afghanistan. See also LMOONZ.

NIMROZE (PROVINCE). The second largest province in Afghanistan, it is situated in the extreme southwestern part of the country. It is marked by salt marshes, desert, and a wind which blows for four months ("the wind of 120 days"). The province of Nimroze has the smallest population per square mile in Afghanistan. It is crossed by three major rivers: the Farah Rud, Khash Rud, and the Helmand Rivers, all emptying in the Seistan Lake. There is some farm land along the banks of these rivers where cotton is the main agricultural product. Despite the obstacles of climate and topography, efforts are being made to develop the resources of the Nimroze Province.

NOMADS see KUCHIS

NUCLEAR FAMILY. A family type which consists of one set of parents and their children, living in one household. Although the extended family predominates throughout Afghanistan, expressions of the nuclear family are increasingly found in large towns and in the cities of the country.

NURISTAN (AREA). Previously known as Kafiristan, this rugged, well-forested mountain area lies north of Jalalabad. The southern extensions of the Hindu Kush break up the area and the Alishang and Alinghar Rivers cross it and flow into the Kabul River. These rivers, used for the transportation of timber, are of great importance because much of the country's forestry production is carried on in the Asmar Forest which lies in the foothills of the Hindu Kush.

NURISTAN (DISTRICT). An administrative division in the province of Laghman in east central Afghanistan. The people are excellent wood carvers. They are well-known for a variety of unique features, including their round woolen hats; their homes, which are made of pine beams and stone

and are two-story structures; their use of tables
and chairs, some of leather and some wood carved;
their wooden beds, and their windows facing east
and west in the rooms. Large carved wooden
horsemen were often placed over graves in this
area, and efforts are being made by the government to keep this art from disappearing.

NURISTANI   see   ETHNIC GROUPS;   LANGUAGES

-O-

OXUS BASIN.   This basin is formed by the Amu Darya
River.   Snows formed in the Pamir and the Hindu
Kush Mountain Ranges feed the entire basin.   The
Amu Darya River rises in the Parmir plateau and
flows westward.   See also AMU DARYA RIVER.

OXUS RIVER.   Ancient name for Amu Darya.   See
also AMU DARYA RIVER and RIVERS.

-P-

PAGHMAN.   A very popular resort town about 12 miles
west of Kabul.   The Paghman Valley floor is about
8,000 feet in altitude and affords cooler weather
during the hot summer months.   Public and private gardens and recreation areas are extensive.
Some of the modernistic structures built by the
reform-minded King Amanullah Khan are located
in Paghman.   For residents of Kabul during Fridays and other holidays, Pahman is a popular
place to spend a few comfortable, cool, and
pleasant days and nights.

PAGHMAN DISTRICT   see   KABUL (PROVINCE)

PAHLAWANI   see   GAMES AND SPORTS

PAKTHIA (PROVINCE).   A province located in southeast Afghanistan.   Its capital is Gardaiz and it is the 17th largest province in size. This is a very mountainous area of the country. It also has hundreds of thousands of acres of virgin timber including pine, willow, spruce, mahogany, and evergreen trees. This area until quite recently has been isolated and nearly inaccessible.

There is some agricultural activity, with the major crops being wheat, corn, barley, and other grains, and citrus fruits. Many agricultural programs are now underway to teach new methods of farming and to develop new crops.

The two main urban centers of the province are Gardaiz and Khosth and each still has the atmosphere of a quiet, rural area.

PALAW. This word is the most common reference to any rice dish in Afghanistan. Essentially, it involves steamed rice, and often it is served as the main dish in a meal or a ceremonial feast. See also FOOD.

PALEOLITHIC. The "Old Stone Age." It refers to the period from 500,000 to 1,500,000 years ago. Crude stone tools characterize the implements of this period and hunting populations characterize the society. Some archaeological sites provide evidence of Paleolithic societies in Afghanistan.

PAMIR KNOT. The knot-like mountain ranges in the Pamir area which rise out of the Qaraqurom, Qunlum, and Himalayan Mountains, and shift the direction of mountain ranges from southeast-northwest to northeast-southwest through Afghanistan. See also GEOGRAPHY.

PAMIR PLATEAU. The highest plateau in northeast Afghanistan. It is known as the "Roof of the World." The average elevation of its sloping sides is about 10,000 feet.

PAMIR RIVER. A river in the Wakhan corridor of Afghanistan which follows a 65-mile course before uniting with the Wakhan River at Qala Panja to form the Panj River.

PANJ RIVER. The confluence of the Wakhan River and
the Pamir River at Qala Panja form this river
which is one of the headstreams of the Amu Darya
River. The Panj River follows a 400-mile course,
then unites with the Vakhsh River from the U.S.S.R.
to form the Amu Darya River. See also WAKHAN
RIVER and PAMIR RIVER.

PANJSHER RIVER. Rising in the Hindu Kush, this
river flows southeasterly for 100 miles. During
its course it is joined by the Ghorband River and
30 miles east of Kabul they join the Kabul River.
See also RIVERS.

PARALLEL-COUSIN MARRIAGE. A marriage pattern
whereby children of two brothers or two sisters
marry. This pattern of marriage is common
throughout Afghanistan. Preference is given to a
man marrying his father's brother's daughter or
his mother's sister's daughter. This pattern of
marriage is particularly designed to facilitate the
cohesiveness of the property held by the groom
and his patrilineage. Although this is a preferen-
tial mode of marriage, cross-cousin and outlineage
and out-clan marriages are now the most common
among the societies of Afghanistan.

PAROPAMISUS MOUNTAINS. This mountain range extends from the northwest spurs of the Kohe Baba
range toward the border of Iran. It runs for about
300 miles and is the northern edge of the Hari
Rud River Valley. A height of about 11,000 feet
is reached northeast of Herat. The Ardewan Pass,
an important trade route, cuts through here at
5,250 feet. Nearby, the Zarmast Pass, at an
elevation of 7,774 feet, also crosses the range.

PARWAN (PROVINCE). Ranked 22nd in size among the
provinces of Afghanistan, it is one of the most
productive regions for viticulture. With the completion of the Salang Pass, Parwan has become a
crossroads for commercial activity and tourism.
The province is primarily an agricultural region,
growing wheat and barley. It is one of the most

mountainous regions in the country, and its valleys attract tourists and commercial interests. Parwan is also well known for its mulberries and a variety of other fruits. See also CHARIKAR.

PASTORAL NOMADS see KUCHIS

PATRIARCHY. The decision-making process in most Afghan societies is in the hands of one or more males. The most important decisions are made by the eldest male members of an Afghan family. Thus the patriarch of an Afghan family makes the important decisions about the status and well-being of the family.

PATRILOCAL POST-MARITAL RESIDENCE. A pattern of residence (common in Afghanistan) whereby the groom and his wife live with the groom's paternal relatives after marriage (preferably the groom's father or his eldest brother).

PAWINDAS see KUCHIS

PAYGHLA. A term of address for unmarried girls. Although the word is derived from Pushtu, it has a universal meaning throughout all Afghan ethnic groups.

POLITICAL ORGANIZATION AND INTERNAL ADMINISTRATION. Afghanistan is a republic with twenty-eight administrative provincial units. The head of the government is the president of the republic. A cabinet and council of ministers serve as the heads of the respective ministries and as consultants to the President, often occupying more than one position. A Revolutionary Council, composed of both military men and civilians, leads the revolution to bring about the republican regime, and is the supreme body which oversees the affairs of the state. The President of the republic is in charge of military, foreign, and internal affairs of Afghanistan. The Republic of Afghanistan was established on July 17, 1973. General Mohammed

Daud is the President and Premier of Afghanistan. Provincial governments are responsible to the central government. Each provincial administration has a representative of the central ministries in the central national government, and is accountable to the central national ministries. The Ministry of Internal Affairs is in charge of appointments of provincial administrative heads, and is the channel through which specialized divisions of the provincial government are accountable to their respective ministries on the national level.

POLYGYNY. A situation where one marries more than one wife. Under Islamic law, a Muslim may marry four wives simultaneously. Although most Afghans live in monogamous families, some still practice polygyny. Since the acquisition of multiple wives requires wealth, polygyny is most common among the well-to-do Afghans. The Afghan government has laws under consideration which will abolish polygyny.

POPULATION DISTRIBUTION. In 1970 the population of Afghanistan was divided into the following general categories:

Total	16.09 million
Nomads	3.08 million
Rural (agricultural)	11.89 million
Urban (cities and towns)	1.96 million

A complete and thorough census of Afghanistan has never been conducted. The above figures are approximations provided by the Ministry of Planning of Afghanistan.

POSTEEN. A heavy knee-length sheepskin coat worn by Afghans during very cold weather. Posteens are often embroidered and the garments, originally made of sheepskin, are commonly of fox fur. The city of Ghazni is known for its fine Posteens.

POSTEENCHA. A sheepskin (sometimes fox fur) waist-length coat made to be worn in cold weather. They are made mostly in Ghazni, usually with intricate embroidery work.

POULLADA, LEON. A contemporary American author who has spent many years in Afghanistan. He has published extensively on the history of Afghanistan. Leon Poullada is among the leaders of those who have encouraged institutional and organized study and research in and about Afghanistan. See also Bibliography.

PRAYER see DAILY PRAYERS

PRE-HISTORY. Much is still unknown about the early history of this area of the world, but the western part of the Iranian plateau has been inhabited since the Paleolithic period and further study will likely establish Neolithic settlements as well. Some believe that the Iranian plateau was the area where animals were first domesticated and where agriculture began.
    The oldest known sculpture found in Asia was located in north Afghanistan. It is an old man's head sculpted on an oblong limestone pebble in an upper-Paleolithic level, dating to ca. 20,000 years ago.
    Painted pottery dating to the 4th millennium B.C. has also been found. The existence of agriculture at a very early time is supported by over seventy remaining varieties of wheat.

PRESIDENT MOHAMMED DAUD. General Mohammed Daud served Afghanistan as premier from 1953 to 1963. During this period the five-year economic development plans were initiated. The operational dimension of these plans are the best examples of what Afghans can do to improve their socio-cultural lot. Afghanistan has not seen another similar period of continuous progress and development. The results of the efforts of General Mohammed Daud's term in office as premier are beginning to show in many dimensions of the political, economic, social, and cultural life of the Afghan society. After the revolution of July 17, 1973, when Afghanistan was proclaimed a republic, the national revolutionary council elected him to the presidency of the Afghan Republic, as well as to the posts of premiership and foreign minister of Afghanistan.

PROPHET MOHAMMED see ISLAM

PUL. An Afghan monetary unit equal to one one-hundredth (1/100) of an afghani. See also CURRENCY.

PULE ALAM. Capital of Logar Province. Also called Baraki Barak, Pule Alam is an agricultural center serving as the administrative center of Logar Province. It is located about 25 miles south of Kabul. Pule Alam serves as the major checkpoint for the nomads who enter Afghanistan from its eastern border. The town also serves as a commercial-market center for the province of Logar.

PULE KHUMRI. A model town built around the textile mills, it is situated about 145 miles north of Kabul. The town is accessible by a modern highway. Pule Khumri has a population of about 25,000. A modern hotel and many ethnic restaurants are available in the town. Pule Khumri is an important stopping point on the way from Kabul to the northern provinces. There are hydroelectric, cement, and textile factories in or close to the town. In addition, there are several agricultural experimental farms located near the city, and a coal mining site is not far away.

PUSHTU see LANGUAGES

PUSHTUN see ETHNIC GROUPS

PUSHTUNWALI. A most prominent cultural value configuration and code of conduct among the Pushtuns. It is the code of an independent and individualistic people who live hard and demanding lives. It sets up strict patterns of conduct and swift punishment for the transgressors. Its most important elements are badal (q.v.), blood revenge; melmastia (q.v.), the obligation of hospitality and the protection given each guest; and nanawati (q.v.), the right of asylum and the obligation to accept a truce offer.

-Q-

QABILA. An Arabic term widely used in Afghanistan. It refers to a tribe or a sociological grouping of several clans who are widely dispersed and claim to have a common heroic (and sometimes mythical) person as their ancestor.

QALAI BOST. A geographical allusion to the ruined city of historical Bost. It is located at the point where the waters of the Arghandab, Tarnak, and Arghastan Rivers meet.

QALAI NAW. Capital of Badghis Province, it is located about 95 miles northeast of Herat and about 180 miles southwest of Maimana. This is a relatively new town, and its bazaars and market place are active places for commerce for the surrounding agricultural population. Uzbeks are predominant among the population of Qalai Naw and the Badghis Province. The town is accessible by secondary roads open to automobiles and lorries.

QALAI QAISAR   see   GHOR (PROVINCE)

QALAT. Capital of Zabul Province. It is located about 85 miles east of Qandahar, and about 220 miles southwest of Kabul. The town is the center of the Ghilzai Pushtun Tribe, the largest Pushtun tribal grouping in Afghanistan. Because of this, the town is also called Qalat-i-Ghilzai (Fort of the Ghilzai). The famous and large 18th century fort of the Ghilzais is located outside the town. In addition to being the administrative center of the

Zabul Province, Qalat is a major point on the
route from Kabul to Qandahar as a commercial
center. Qalat is also famous for the varied and
large melons produced in the Zabul Province.

QAMARI CALENDAR see CALENDAR

QANAT. Underground water canals. They consist of a
line of wells or shafts connected by tunnels to intercept the water table. The Qanat system brings
water to the surface for use in irrigation. Qanats
are mostly found in the desert and semi-desert
areas of Afghanistan. The Qanat is called Karez
in Pushtu.

QANDAHAR (CITY). The second largest city in Afghanistan, Qandahar, the capital of Qandahar Province,
is an agricultural and industrial center. It is the
center of activity for the region south of the Hindu
Kush. It has an international airport and there
are major roads leading from Qandahar west to
Herat and east to Kabul.
   Haravati and the Rig Veda Surashuti are
names given to this area in the Avesta. During
the time of Alexander, the city built here was an
agricultural village. Remains include sundried
brick, terra cotta bull figurines, stone hoes, and
awls. An urban period--later in its history--was
a time in which alabaster work reached a high
point.
   In 1747 in this city, Ahmad Shah Durrani
was chosen the first Supreme Chief of Afghanistan.
Many monuments in and around the city mark important events in the history of Afghanistan.

QANDAHAR (PROVINCE). A province in south-central
Afghanistan with an area of 45,333 sq. km. Its
capital is Qandahar (q.v.). Orchards cover the
fertile land--grapes being the principal crop.
Raisins as well as grapes are exported. The
Abjush raisin is the most popular. Qandahar
pomegranates--some reaching 18 centimeters in
diameter are grown along the Arghandab River

and are sent to many parts of this area.
Unirrigated land is used to graze sheep.
Mills in Qandahar process the high quality wool
from the sheep into cloth. A fruit canning company--the Qandahar Fruit Company--processes
fruit in the province. See also QANDAHAR (CITY)
and HISTORY.

QARAQUL see QARAQUL SHEEP

QARAQUL SHEEP. These animals are raised principally in the province of Fariab to provide the
famous Qaraqul pelts (misleadingly called "Persian
Lamb"). There are now over thirty cooperatives
to handle the raising and trading of these animals.
Qaraqul pelts are exported in large quantities to
Europe and the United States.

QARYAH. A Dari term usually meaning a village, community, or a small settlement. See also KELAY.

QAUM. A general term used in Afghanistan to refer to
one's clan or ethnic group. In some instances it
may refer to lineage, or place of origin.

QAYMAQ. Lumps of milk curds with a distinctive salty
flavor. Qaymaq is usually eaten with sugar, generally for breakfast. Sometimes Qaymaq is added
to green tea and flavored with cardamom (Qaymaq-Chai) and served at special occasions such as weddings.

QAYYUM, NAWABZADA ABDUL. A distinguished Pushtun who, along with an Englishman by the name of
Roos-Keppel, founded the Islamia College, now the
University of Peshawar. He also pushed for a
program of gradual emancipation of the North-West
Frontier in the early 1930's.

QAZI. A judge in the courts of Afghanistan who handles
both secular and religious cases. Traditionally the
Qazi has had little or no formal training, except
a general understanding of the Quran. Presently

all Qazis must go through formal training in theology and sociology in learning institutions subsidized by the Afghan Government.

QISHLAQ. The winter headquarters of most nomadic and semi-nomadic groups in Afghanistan. Here the semi-nomads grow some crops, and after reaping these crops in autumn, they stay throughout the winter months, and then move on to their summer pasturelands. See also IYLAQ.

QIZIL QALA   see   GREAT NORTH ROAD

QIZILBASH. Primarily an urban group scattered throughout Afghanistan. They are the descendants of the military and administrative personnel left behind by the Persian King Nadir Shah Afshar in the 18th century. They speak Dari, and belong to the shi'a sect of Islam.

QOLE NADER. A small Buddhist monastery at Kapisa (of the Kushan era), dating to the 2nd-3rd centuries A. D. Its most important feature is the complete reliquary which was discovered intact.

QORMA. A most popular meat dish in Afghanistan. It is comprised of either stewed meat alone or a stewed meat dish with a vegetable or fruit.

QRUT. Dried cheese eaten as sour cream after the dried chunks of Qrut have been softened in water.

QUNDUZ (CITY). Capital of Qunduz Province. The town is located about 215 miles north of Kabul and is reached by paved highway. Qunduz is a fast-growing agricultural and industrial center in Afghanistan. The town is the home of a 300 year-old Masjid and a historic citadel. A large company which participates in raising, ginning, and exporting cotton has its headquarters and factories in Qunduz.

QUNDUZ (PROVINCE). A province located in north-

central Afghanistan. Its capital is Qunduz and it
ranks 24th in size among the provinces of the
country. Cotton, vegetable oil, and silk are important to the economy of the province. For
decades Qunduz was the only major cotton producer in the country. One important company,
Spin Zar, which raises, gins, and exports cotton
and produces edible oil and soap, has its headquarters in Qunduz. The province has gained
much in the way of buildings, the construction of
hotels and theaters, street improvements, as well
as the many jobs which the Spin Zar Company has
created.
   The handwoven, colorful cloth produced by
the silk weavers is sought after for kerchiefs and
dresses. Though much of the land is flat and has
an abundance of vegetation, mountain ranges are
also found. In the west on the Kara-Bator Range,
are found many pistachio and almond trees. The
Anbar Koh and the Khwaja Abdul Kasim Mountains
are located in the northern part of this province.

QUNDUZ RIVER. The major tributary of the Amu Darya
River (q.v.), it follows a 250-mile course through
the Bamyan and the Shikari Valleys in the northern
foothills of the Hindu Kush. Its waters are important to the agricultural area in the Northern
Plains near and around Qunduz. It joins the Amu
Darya on the USSR border. See also RIVERS.

QUR'AN. The holy book of Muslims. It contains the
revealed word of Allah through the Prophet
Mohammed.

-R-

RABIA BALKHI. A poetess from the ancient city of
Balkh. Afghanistan, in 1966, celebrated the
thousandth anniversary of her death. According
to legend, this daughter of Amir learned to write
poetry among literary circles of the court. Her
brother became jealous and killed her father and

attempted to kill her lover Baktash. It goes on to say that Rabia died while in prison, writing poetry on the wall in her blood.

RADIO AFGHANISTAN. The major radio station in Afghanistan. Its shortwave transmitters are powered by 50 and 100 kilowatts. Radio Afghanistan also has a 20-kilowatt medium-wave transmitter. In addition to programs in major languages for broadcast in Afghanistan, Radio Afghanistan broadcasts programs on the short wave band in Arabic, English, German, Russian, Turkish, and Urdu.

RAMADZAN. The lunar month of fasting. During Ramadzan, government and business offices are open for one-half day during the morning hours. Afghans, like all other Muslims, cannot eat or have sexual intercourse from sunrise to sunset during this time. Smoking and drinking are also prohibited. Only adults are required to fast. See also FIVE PILLARS OF ISLAM.

RECITATION. Stating publicly that "there is no God but Allah and Mohammed is His Prophet." These are the first words a newborn child must hear. A Muslim, in good faith and in a state of ritual cleanliness must, at least once in a lifetime, recite the above words (preferably in Arabic). See also FIVE PILLARS OF ISLAM.

REGISTAN. A desert region of vast plains south of Qandahar of mixed sand, loam, clay, and gravel which, along with the Dashte Margo area, comprises about 15,000 square miles of barren land. It lies between 1,500 and 2,000 feet above sea level and is about 150 miles wide. Important trade routes cross them from Qandahar through Spin Boldak in southern Afghanistan. The Helmand River Valley on the west separates this from the Dashte Margo Desert.

RELIGION see ISLAM

REPUBLIC OF AFGHANISTAN. On July 17, 1973 A.D., the Afghan monarchy was overthrown, and the country was declared a republic. The Revolutionary Council, on that day, elected General Mohammed Daud as Premier, Founder, and first President of the Republic of Afghanistan. The republican regime of Afghanistan has inaugurated new developmental plans for the country and has accelerated the pace of other developmental projects. Progressive social, cultural, and judicial reforms, serving the aspirations and needs of the Afghan people, have been proposed and implemented. Cultural, commercial, and diplomatic relationships with friendly nations are maintained. The Republican Government of Afghanistan particularly encourages visits to Afghanistan by scholars and others interested in the natural beauty of the country, and/or in carrying out responsible, professional, and scholastic research and study of the Afghan society and culture.

RIG VEDA. One of the oldest collections of hymns, the composition of which is attributed to the second half of the millennium. These hymns were composed by the priests of the early Aryans who entered India through Afghanistan in the second millennium B.C. and were handed down by word of mouth, and early in the first millennium B.C. were collected and arranged. This great collection of hymns is the Rig Veda, still in theory the earliest account of the history of the Aryans.

RIG VEDA SURASHUTI see QANDAHAR (CITY)

RIVERS. The water drainage system of Afghanistan is landlocked. Only a few rivers, all in the eastern part of the country and drained mainly by the Kabul River, reach the ocean after emptying into the Indus River. Most of the rivers and streams end in shallow desert lakes or oases inside or outside Afghanistan's boundaries. About ten per cent of the surface area of eastern Afghanistan has no rivers. In the western part of the Northern

Plains many rivers disappear in the soil before emptying into the Amu Darya. In the west the sandy deserts along the Iranian frontier have no watercourses. Nearly half of Afghanistan is drained by watercourses south of the Hindu Kush mountain range, and half of this area is drained by the Helmand River system. The Amu Darya, the country's other major river, has the next largest drainage area.

Melting glaciers feed the rivers in the northeast. The water yield of rivers in the rest of the country depends on the seasonal pattern of rainfall, snowfall, or on sudden torrential rains. Rivers rise at the end of the winter. Their minimum yield is at the end of the summer or the beginning of autumn. Rivers which spring in the glaciers of the Pamir Knot or in Nuristan have a minimum yield in the winter during severe freezing. The maximum yield occurs in July and August when the snows have melted. The waters of Afghanistan can be divided into four river systems:

1. The 1,655-mile-long Amu Darya originates in the glaciers of the Pamir Knot. About 600 miles of its upper course constitutes the Afghanistan-USSR border. Nearly half of the surface area of its tributaries are in Afghanistan. Two of the larger tributaries, the Kokcha and the Qunduz, rise in the mountains of Badakhshan. Along the banks of the Amu Darya there is often abundant vegetation of trees and bushes. During the 1960's attempts were made to exploit the navigational potential of the Amu Darya (in favor of Afghanistan) by improving some of the existing ports on the Afghan side of the river.

2. Two important rivers of the northern and northwestern part of Afghanistan are the Murghab and Hari Rud. Their respective drainage areas are separated by the Parapamisus and Firoz Koh mountain chains. The Murghab flows about 200 miles in a northwesterly direction from the eastern end of the Firoz Koh before entering the USSR. It drains the valleys of the Parapamisus

and Bandi-Turkistan mountain ranges. The Hari Rud, rising at an altitude of about 9,000 feet on the western slopes of the Kohe Baba Range, takes a steady westerly course. The river goes through the high valleys and across a broad plateau valley and flows south of Herat through a fertile oasis district which depends on its waters for irrigation. About 80 miles west of Herat, the Hari Rud turns north and constitutes the border between Afghanistan and Iran for 65 miles before it crosses the confluence of the Afghan-USSR boundaries.

3. In the eastern region, the Kabul River, flowing eastward from the Kohe Mazar chain, has the largest drainage area. Its major tributary on the south is the Logar River. On the north are three additional tributaries--the Panjsher, the Alingar, and the Kunar. They originate in the northeastern slopes of the Hindu Kush. The Kabul River, after traversing the capital city, turns southeast, crossing the eastern border, and becomes a major tributary of the Indus River. The Kabul River has a steady flow of water, and, together with its tributaries, is used intensively for irrigation.

4. The Helmand is the major river in the southwest. With its many tributaries, the most important of which is the Arghandab River, it drains more than 100,000 square miles. Starting some 50 miles west of Kabul in the Kohe Baba mountains, the Helmand is approximately 880 miles long. In the upper and central courses, the river cuts through deep alpine valleys. Before entering the Registan Desert, northwest of Qandahar, the waterflow is collected in a large valley reservoir. A similar reservoir exists on the Helmand's main west-bank tributary, the Arghandab, northeast of Qandahar. The two dams and the irrigation canal systems were constructed by the Helmand-Arghandab Valley Authority (HAVA), the country's major hydrological project.

Below its confluence with the Arghandab, the Helmand becomes a slow, meandering stream without affluence. It crosses the Registan and Dashte

Margo Deserts and continues its course to the desert lakes of the Seistan depression. Three major rivers form part of the Helmand drainage basin: the Khash Rud, Farah Rud, and Harut Rud, all originating in the Bande Bayan and Kasa Murgh mountain ranges.

ROBERTSON, GEORGE SCOTT. A British military officer who, in the 19th century, carried out pioneering research among the Nuristanis in Afghanistan. His publications on this large ethnic group are primary sources about the society and culture of the Nuristanis. See also Bibliography.

RODAKI see HISTORY--Islamic Period

ROGHAN ZARD. Called ghwari in Pushtu, it is clarified butter used in the cooking of most Afghan food. The Hazarajat area is known for producing the largest quantity and the best quality of Roghan Zard. It is sometimes referred to as simply roghan.

ROOS-KEPPEL. A dedicated and devoted Englishman who, along with a distinguished Pushtun, Nawabzada Abdul Qayyum, founded the Islamia College, now the University of Peshawar.

RUBAND. The Zoroastrian term for the little veil used to cover the nose and mouth while in the presence of a sovereign one or when reading the Avesta. In the Avesta itself, the veil was known as panam or paiti-dana. This practice has continued in Afghanistan in a modified way. In the presence of elders, strangers, or an important personage, some rural Afghans cover parts of their face. The Ruband is probably a logical antecedent for the contemporary chadari. See also CHADARI.

RULERS see DURRANI DYNASTIES

RUZA. The Afghan term for fasting. See also RAMADZAN.

-S-

SAFED KOH MOUNTAIN RANGE (EASTERN). A major range in the eastern part of Afghanistan. It runs westward from the Peshawar district along the southern edge of the Kabul River Valley, to the Logar River Valley south of Kabul. The highest peak is Sikaram, which is 15,260 feet high. It is crossed by two main passes, the Khyber Pass (3,500 feet) and the Paiwar Pass (8,531 feet). See also KHYBER PASS.

SAFED KOH MOUNTAIN RANGE (WESTERN). An extension of the Kohe Babe Range, it extends for about 100 miles west along the south side of the Hari Rud River Valley. Just northwest of Shahrak the range reaches an elevation of around 10,000 feet.

SALANG PASS see GEOGRAPHY (Central Highlands)

SALANG TUNNEL. The Great North Road--a paved highway connecting Kabul with the Afghan-Russian border port of Qizil Qala on the Amu Darya--passes through this tunnel. It is about 11,000 feet in length. The tunnel and the highway were built with the cooperation of the Ministry of Public Works of Afghanistan and the Institute of Techno-Export of the Soviet Union.

SAMANGAN (PROVINCE). A province located in north-central Afghanistan. Its capital is Aibak and it ranks 16th in area among the country's provinces.
Important products of Samangan include melons and other fruits, coal and iron. Major coal mines are Shabashak and Dakne Tour (in 12 seams of workable thickness). Hard coal and coke seams are in abundance at Shabashak. The coal's caloric value is 76,000-83,000. Coal reserves of the workable seams are 44 million tons in geological reserves, and of the entire area are estimated at more than 73 million tons. Over 25 tons a day are mined at Dakne Tour, about

50 miles from Shabashak. Mazare Sharif is the destination of most of this. The raising and training of Buzkashi horses is also important here. See also AIBAK.

SAMOVAR. Samovars are of Tartar origin and became popular in northern Afghanistan in the early 18th century. Samovars are metal urns made for brewing and making tea. Most that are found in Afghanistan today date from the 19th century and are usually of brass, although copper and silver examples are also known. In the trunk or base of the samovar there is an open center tube extending from the top down into the main body. This tube, which rests upon a small iron grate at the bottom, is filled with charcoal or live coal and acts as a central heater to keep the water hot. Actually the word "samovar" is Russian and means "self boiler," and that is exactly what the samovar does, boil the water and keep it hot. Samovars of different sizes and different styles are found throughout Afghanistan's scores of chaikhanas or tea houses, in villages, towns and cities. Earlier samovars are heavier in weight and usually have handles of wood and metal, while those of a later vintage are lighter and usually have handles made completely of metal.

SANA'I. A Sufi philosopher-poet of the 12th century during the period of the Ghaznavid Dynasty. He wrote mystical epics and other poetic works. He was born in Ghazni and was nurtured at the courts of Ghaznavi Emperors. He is buried in Ghazni and his shrine lies just outside the northeastern part of Ghazni.

SANDALI. A wooden table-like piece placed over a charcoal brazier (manqal) with a blanket spread over it so that it drapes over and extends over the floor. In winter months, whole Afghan families sit around the Sandali, covering their legs, arms and much of their bodies under the blanket to absorb the heat.

SARE DAURA. A large plateau located about one mile southeast of the city of Qunduz in the province of Qunduz. Buzkashi games are popular here. An airport is situated closeby.

SAYR. An Afghan unit of weight equal to about 15.6 pounds.

SAYYID. Religious leaders who claim descent from the Prophet Mohammed. They are found all over Afghanistan, and are usually held in esteem in the communities in which they reside. One of their main functions is to prescribe amulets and to serve as mediators in cases of local political conflict.

SAYYID JAMALUDDIN AFGHANI. A 19th century leader of religious and political reform in the Moslem world. He was a great scholar from the Kunar Province in Afghanistan. He spent much of his time outside Afghanistan, in Egypt, Europe and Turkey. He propounded many reforms in Islamic theology and was an outspoken anti-traditionalist. He died in Turkey. His remains were transferred to Afghanistan after World War II and are buried in a magnificent tomb on the campus of Kabul University.

SCHURMANN, H. F. An American scholar who did extensive work among the Moghuls of Afghanistan. His writings on the Moghuls are a primary source of material for students and scholars interested in the ethnology of Afghanistan. See also Bibliography.

SEISTAN. A lacustrine depression south of Dashte Margo which extends into Iran. During dry seasons some of the land is used for raising cereals and cotton. Much of the land, however, is scrub and marsh. The Helmand River and its tributaries water the area and most of the people living in Seistan live in the oases of the Helmand River.

SEISTAN BASIN. Located in Southwestern Afghanistan, this basin is marked by a lacustrine depression.

It is formed by the Helmand, the Farah Rud, the Adreskan and the Khash Rud Rivers. The Seistan Basin opens up into the Seistan Desert and Seistan Lake. The Helmand River and its tributaries (the most important being the Arghandab and the Turnak) provide water for many irrigation projects. The Khash Rud River rises in the Siah Koh and empties into the Seistan Lake. The Farah Rud rises in the Siah Koh also but disappears in the Seistan Desert. The Adreskan River flows into the Humaira Saliari Lake in the Seistan Depression. See also HELMAND RIVER, FARAH RUD RIVER, HAMUN-I-HELMAND LAKE.

SEISTAN LAKE   see   SEISTAN BASIN

SHAFI'AI   see   HANAFI

SHAGHALAY. An Afghan title equivalent to "Sir" or "Mr." It is primarily used for government officials and other dignitaries, Afghan or non-Afghan.

SHAH FULADI PEAK   see   KOHE BABA MOUNTAIN RANGE

SHAH RUKH. The youngest son of Timure Lung (Tamurlane), a conqueror of Herat, who did much to rebuilt the city of Herat. This famous Central Asian ruler was in power from 1404 to 1447. His wife, Gawhar-Shad, ruled with him throughout Afghanistan, India, and most of Iran and Muslim Soviet Central Asia.

SHAHEED   see   ZIARAT

SHALWAR. Baggy, bloomer-like trousers worn by rural Afghans. They are loosely tailored and homemade, designed for both men and women. Their use is common throughout Afghanistan.

SHAMSHIR GHAR. "Cave of the Swords," it is a unique archaeological cave site about fifteen miles west of Qandahar. Shamshir Ghar has yielded a four-period ceramic and stratigraphic sequence of three basic pre-Islamic occupations: I. pre-Kushan, pre-1st century B.C.; II. Kushan, 1st century B.C. to mid-3rd century A.D.; and III. Kushano-Sasanian. These major cultural levels were periodically occupied from the mid-3rd to late 7th centuries A.D. See also ARCHAEOLOGY.

SHAMSI CALENDAR. The official solar calendar of Afghanistan. Its first month begins about March 21st. See also CALENDAR.

SHARIA. A body of Islamic laws derived from the revelations of the Qur'an. The Shariat applies to Muslims not only when they come before a judge (Qazi) to obtain a decision but also in their daily activities, telling them what their religious duties are, what to eat and drink, how to treat their families and how to give gifts and bequeath possessions.

SHEBERGHAN. Capital of Jozjan Province. Located about 130 miles northeast of Maimana and about 85 miles west of Mazare Sharif, Sheberghan was once the capital of an independent province of Soviet Central Asia. Since becoming the capital of Jozjan Province, Sherberghan has enjoyed a boom in new residential and private buildings. In addition to being an administrative center, Sheberghan is also an important commercial and trading center in northern Afghanistan.

SHI'A. One of the two major sects of Islam. See also ISLAM.

SIAH KOH MOUNTAIN RANGE. Extends from north-central Afghanistan westward and disappears before reaching the western boundary of Afghanistan with Iran. Major iron ore deposits are found in this range. At its highest point the Siah Koh rises to about 12,000 feet.

SIAH KOH PEAK. A mountain peak located on the

Iranian border in southern Afghanistan which is
4,262 feet in elevation. It is not a part of the
Siah Koh Mountain Range.

SIDDHARTHA   see   GAUTAMA BUDDHA

SIKH   see   ETHNIC GROUPS

SISTAN   see   SEISTAN, SEISTAN BASIN and SEISTAN LAKE

SPIN ZAR COMPANY   see   QUNDUZ (PROVINCE)

STATE EMBLEM. The state emblem of the Republic
of Afghanistan constitutes two ears of wheat,
mehrab and mumber, an eagle and a rising sun.
The ears of wheat which form a circle from two
sides of the emblem encircling other parts of the
emblem symbolizes the fact that Afghanistan is an
agricultural country. At the bottom of the wheat
circle are the words "Republic of Afghanistan" in
Pushtu and the day, month, and year (July 17,
1973 in Pushtu script, solar month, and year) of
the revolution which established the Republic of
Afghanistan.
   The mehrab and mumbar (symbols of the
place of prostration of Muslims and the pulpit from
which believers are invited to seek the way of salvation) stand in the middle of the emblem.
   The eagle symbolizes Afghanistan as a
mountainous country, and that, like eagles, the
people of Afghanistan have defended and will defend
their country against conquerors and intruders.

SUDDHODHANA   see   GAUTAMA BUDDHA

SUFI. Muslim religious mystics found throughout Afghanistan. They lead a life of isolated contemplation.
This type of religious experience is characterized
by nonattachment to material things, concentration,
and meditation directed toward identification of the
individual with the divine essence of Allah. Its
attraction persists in the country and it is not

considered out of the ordinary even for an educated government official, a teacher, or a wealthy aristocrat to give up his post and become a sufi.

SUFISM. Refers to the sufi-style of life and religious experience. See also SUFI.

SULAIMAN MOUNTAIN RANGE. Located in southern and southeastern Afghanistan it extends beyond the boundaries of Afghanistan. The eastern extension of this range separates the Indus Basin from Afghan territory.

SULTAN MAHMOOD GHAZNAVI. The most famous of the Ghaznavid rulers, he extended his dominion from Afghanistan to the Punjab in India and beyond. With his accumulated wealth, he built up his capital of Ghazni into a great center of art, commerce, and literature. It housed some of the loveliest buildings of the day and became an important center for poets and scholars from many parts of the world. He was also known as Mahmood the Iconoclast, or Image Breaker. He is buried in Ghazni and his tomb attracts many visitors for a variety of reasons ranging from healing to paying genuine political and ideological homage. See also HISTORY --Ghaznavid Period.

SUNNI. One of the two major sects of Islam which is the most common in Afghanistan. See also ISLAM.

-T-

TA'AWIZ   see   AMULET

TAHARIDS   see   HISTORY--Islamic Period

TAJIK   see   ETHNIC GROUPS

TAJIKI   see   LANGUAGES

TAKHAR (PROVINCE). A province located in northeast

Afghanistan. Its capital is Taloqan. It ranks 15th in size among the provinces of Afghanistan. An important mineral resource of the area is its salt. Two-thirds of all the salt used in the country comes from here. Grains, fruit, and nuts (almonds and pistachio), as well as cotton, are important crops. The cotton seeds and sesame seeds are the source for vegetable oil which is now in great demand. The mountains afford a good water supply for the grain and fruit crops.

TALOQAN. Capital of Takhar Province. A small, isolated administrative center, it is important as a center of commerce and trade to the agriculturalists of nearby towns. Taloqan is situated in a beautiful mountainous valley and is the staging point for mountaineers and sightseers.

TAMERLANE see TIMURE LUNG

TANDUR. Distinctive bread ovens found throughout the country. They are made of half-baked pottery and are buried in the ground with wood fire at the bottom. Flattened dough is slapped against the inner wall of the Tandur for baking.

TANOOR see NAN and TANDUR

TARNAK RIVER. This river, which begins its course 45 miles southwest of Ghazni, follows a southwesterly direction for 210 miles until it joins the Arghastan River about 17 miles southwest of Qandahar. It joins the Helmand River at Qala Bist and ultimately empties into the Seistan lacustrine depression in the south. See also HELMAND RIVER and SEISTAN BASIN.

TASHQURGHAN. Situated about 235 miles north of Kabul in the Province of Samangan, Tashqurghan is an important commercial town famous for its fruits, especially figs and pomegranates, and its handicrafts, particularly ironwork and lacquerware. The town is a major trans-shipment center of the northern provinces of Afghanistan. Its bazaars are famous for their variety and abundance of commercial goods throughout the northern part of the country.

TAZI (AFGHAN HOUND) see GAMES AND SPORTS

TEKNONYMY. A system of naming children in Afghanistan. In this system children are referred to as the son or daughter of so and so (their father). Afghan children are not given uniform names when they are born into the same family. Usually people go by a first and sometimes middle name. Only when asked by officials (and ethnographers) will they reveal whose children they are and to which family they belong. In urban areas children of the same father and mother may adopt different last names and record them on official documents. Some large aristocratic urban families are exceptions to this rule. Nevertheless, the best way to identify an Afghan is to ask whose child he or she is.

TIMUR SHAH DURRANI see DURRANI DYNASTY

TIMURE LUNG. Often known, in English, as "Tamerlane," the English term is a corruption of timur leng or timure lung, meaning "Timur the Lame." Born in Kesh, near Samarkand, ca. 1336, he died in Otrar on February 17, 1405. He was a descendant of Chengis Khan and became chief of his tribe, or people, in 1370 after a period of joint rule with his brother, Hussien. Timure Lung took over the chieftainship by having his brother put to death following a short-lived but violent civil war. He subdued Persia and the whole of central Asia from the Great Wall of China to Moscow, and in 1389 invaded India and conquered those lands lying between the Indus and the mouth of the Ganges Rivers. His territorial conquests continued through 1402. In 1404 he commenced preparations for an invasion of China, but died before the event could begin. Although Timure

Lung is commonly alluded to as a barbarian, he was also an able administrator, patron of the arts and sciences and a statesman. He is considered the founder or the first ruler of the Timurid period, the antecedent of the Moghul Dynasty.

TIMURID PERIOD   see   TIMURE LUNG

TIRIN.   Capital of Urozgan Province. Situated at the confluence of the Tirin Rud and Kamisan Rud Rivers, the town of Tirin is primarily a stopping point for camel caravans. The town has a bazaar and a market place. Commerce and trade are organized around agriculture and farm products. Owing to the rough terrain and sometimes impassable road conditions, Tirin is relatively inaccessible.

TOURISM.   The tourist industry has been on the increase ever since new roads, hotels and improved transportation facilities were built in the early 1960's. The Afghan Tourist Organization, with offices in Kabul and at points of entry, provides information, brochures, pamphlets, etc. for those who wish to visit Afghanistan.

TREATY OF GANDAMAK.   A treaty signed in 1879 by Britain and Afghanistan, placing Afghan foreign relations and the Khyber Pass under British control. The treaty was signed at Gandamak. Roads were built and communication networks improved by the British in order to maintain this control. They felt this was crucial to the safety of India.

TURKMAN   see   ETHNIC GROUPS

TURKMANI   see   LANGUAGES

-U-

ULEMA.   Traditionally, the ulema (bodies of religious leaders) in Afghanistan advised the executive and legislative branches on Islamic matters, literally controlling the courts and the schools, as well as watching over and commenting on public and private morality and customs. After General Mohommed Daud (now President of the Republic of Afghanistan) became Prime Minister in 1953, however, the political and judiciary power of the <u>ulema</u> substantially declined.

ULUGH BEG. The grandson of Timure Lung (Tamerlane), he ruled Afghanistan from 1447 to 1449. He was a patron of art and architecture. Ulugh Beg was an astronomer and built a large observatory outside Samarkand and made many contributions to astronomy. See also CHENGIS KHAN.

UNSURI. A poet during the Ghaznavid period. He was one of the creators of the panegyric style of poetry. He was also a moralist and a sufi-philosopher.

UROZGAN (PROVINCE). A province located in central Afghanistan. Its capital is Tirin and it ranks eighth in size in the country. Much of the province is desert and wasteland, making travel by camel often the most practical. Winters are long and harsh with snow beginning to fall in October and lasting until the end of April. During the summer, cereals--wheat, barley, maize, chick beans, millet, and sesame--are raised. Most of the fruits and vegetables must be brought in from other provinces. The Arjestan plateau, surrounded by the Tous Mountains, is typical of the province's terrain. The winters are cold but the summers are mild and pleasant. A small river flowing east to west and the abundant underground springs keep the plateau well watered.

UZBEK see ETHNIC GROUPS

UZBEKI see LANGUAGES

VALUES AND BELIEFS. Islam has penetrated the cultural and social plane of Afghanistan. Cultural values and beliefs revolve around Islamic principles and dicta. If one is to understand the value patterns of Afghans, one must understand Islam. Ethnic and sectarian differences exist, and are primarily expressions of pre-Islamic continuities and of the mode of adaptation of indigenous Afghan communities to Islam. See also FIVE PILLARS OF ISLAM and ISLAM.

VIMA KADPHISES (KADPHISES II). The son of Kajula Kadphises (q.v.), he continued his father's march and completed the conquest of northern India. He was not as successful in his fight with the Chinese, however, and lost a battle with Panchao, which resulted in Aryana paying an annual tribute to the Chinese emperor. He was more successful in his commercial expansion. Great shipments of silk and gems to the Roman Empire brought in quantities of gold. He took the title "King of Kings."

-W-

WAKHAN CORRIDOR. The narrow strip of land extending eastwards from Afghanistan's northeastern corner to the border of Sinkiang, a province of the People's Republic of China. This rugged area is bounded by the Pamir Mountains on the north and the Hindu Kush chain on the Kashmir border to the south. The Wakhan River, 100 miles long, crosses the corridor. The Wakhjir Pass is the major pass across the Hindu Kush into China. Its altitude on the Afghanistan side of the border is 16,150 feet. Kirghiz herdsmen make two 280-mile round trips across this land during the winter from Mulk Ali, their home camp, to Khandad where they purchase necessary supplies. Part of their route is the old Silk Road which was once used by Marco Polo. The temperature may drop to as low as -20°F. Crossing the frozen Wakhan River is just one of the many dangers these people and their camel caravan face. See also ETHNIC GROUPS.

WAKHAN RIVER. A river in the Wakhan corridor of Afghanistan which follows a 100-mile course, then unites with the Pamir River at Qala Panja to form the Panj River. See also PANJ RIVER.

WALI. A governor of an Afghan province. The Walis are appointed by the Central Government of Afghanistan and are responsible to the Premier through the Afghan Ministry of Interior. In their administration they are advised by an elected provincial council.

WARDAK (PROVINCE). A province located in east-central Afghanistan. Its capital is Maidan, and it ranks 20th among Afghan provinces. The "north pole" of Afghanistan--Behsood--is located in Wardak. It is located in the Kohe Baba Mountain Range at an altitude of 9,625 feet. The three main rivers are: the Helmand, about 450 miles long with headwaters on the Kohe Baba; the Maidan, about 300 miles long (a tributary of the Kabul River), beginning on the Onai Pass at an altitude of 10,000 feet; and the Chak, which begins in Behsood and flows to the eastern valley of Wardak. The Jeghatto River was the site of Afghanistan's first hydroelectric dam, which has supplied electricity to Kabul for fifty years. Well-known individuals from this province include a poet (Abdul Ali Mostaghni), a governor of Kabul, and a nuclear physicist.

WARDAK RIVER see LOGAR RIVER

WAZIR. A minister or head of a ministry in the Central-National Cabinet of Afghanistan.

WILAYAT. Afghan term for province. There are twenty-eight provinces in Afghanistan, divided into districts and subdistricts. The term _wilayat_ is derived from Turkish and means "a major administrative unit."

WILBUR, DONALD N. An American author who has written extensively on Afghan culture and society. He is the author of the Afghanistan entry in the Human Relations Area Files (HRAF). See also Bibliography.

WITCHCRAFT. Many non-Islamic practices still continue in Afghanistan. Among them are witchcraft, black magic, shamanism, and varieties of voodoo. Of all these witchcraft is the most common. Witches in Afghanistan are usually old women past childbearing age. Upon confession and public conviction, witches are usually killed. Imitative magic (like produces like) is also practiced by these witches.

WIZARAT. A ministry in the Central Government of Afghanistan in Kabul. There are fourteen ministries comprising the Central Cabinet of the country, which is headed by the Premier. Usually these are appointed posts.

WOLOSWAL. The chief administrator of a woloswali, a district within an Afghan province. They are appointed by the Central Government and are responsible to the head or Wali (q.v.) of their respective province.

WOLOSWALI. An administrative district within a province. Its chief administrator is called woloswal.

-Y-

YAHUD see ETHNIC GROUPS (Jews)

YAQUB IBN LAYTH see HISTORY--Islamic Period

YASODHAMA. Wife of Gautama Buddha (q.v.).

YURT. A light circular tent characteristic of the Central Asian Plains and the nomadic tribesmen of northern Afghanistan. The Yurt is a collapsible

frame structure with a door on the side-wall and
a hole in the conical top to serve as a chimney.
The framework is usually covered with light straw
matting in the summer and with felt in the winter.

-Z-

ZABUL. A province located in south-central Afghanistan.
Its capital in Qalat (q.v.) and it ranks 13th in size
among Afghan provinces. Dry (lalmi) farming is
the major source of income. The lack of adequate
precipitation as well as low lying rivers and per-
petual winds, however, make it a very marginal
business. Almonds, which grow on the mountains
and hills, are exported in great quantity. Gold
has been found recently. The Zabulis are known
best for their excellent horsemanship in the game
of Naizabazi or tent pegging.

ZAHIRUDDIN MOHAMMED BABUR. A descendant of
Chengis Khan, he was the founder of the great
Moghul Empire of India. He conquered Afghanis-
tan and made Kabul his capital. He also went to
India and defeated Ibrahim Lodi, who was the
Afghan king of Delhi.
      Though a strong military leader and soldier,
Babur was a lover of nature, poetry, and litera-
ture. He truly loved the country of Afghanistan
and, upon his request, was buried in the Bagh-i-
Babur, the Garden of Babur, outside the city of
Kabul.

ZAKAT. One of the five tenets of Islam requiring all
Muslims to pay an annual alms tax as a religious
duty. It is used for charitable and religious purposes. See also FIVE PILLARS OF ISLAM.

ZAMEEN DAR. The Afghan term for a landowner.
The Zameen Dar are few in number but hold much
of the agricultural land in Afghanistan. The majority of farm laborers work on the lands of the
Zameen Dar. By virtue of their control and

ownership of the land, the Zameen Dar are influential in community decision-making processes as well as in the resolution of local conflicts, particularly over the distribution of water and over land.

ZANGILAK PEAK see BAND-I-TURKESTAN MOUNTAINS

ZAR GAR. The Afghan term for a "goldsmith." Their shops sell exquisite local jewelry and can be found in the bazaars of larger cities.

ZARANJ. Capital of Nimroze Province (q.v.), Zaranj is a new town built in the southwestern part of Nimroze Province near the Afghan boundary with Iran. Secondary roads connect the town with the major highway network in Afghanistan.

ZIARAT. Almost all villages, peasant communities, towns and cities in Afghanistan have a Ziarat, or shrine to important religious leaders, known and verifiable, or mythical Muslim saints, famous sufis, or shaheeds (Muslim martyrs, particularly those killed in holy wars, jihad, against non-Muslims). Afghans flock in great numbers to these shrines and ask for the intercession of a particular saint, sufi, or religious leader with Allah for specific favors. The favors asked are primarily for curing diseases and fertility. The Ziarat caretakers are given tokens of food or money to insure the fulfillment of the requests. Some shrines are known for particular curing powers for particular diseases, and others are known to have generalized powers.

ZOO. The Kabul Zoo opened in 1967. Built according to modern concepts, the zoo presents Afghanistan's birds and mammals in open, natural settings. As of Spring 1970 there were thirty-six species of mammals, eleven species of birds, and twenty-five species of reptiles and fish. The Kabul Zoo is open during the summer from 8 a.m. to 7 p.m. Winter hours are 9 a.m. to 5 p.m.

There is a nominal admission fee. There is no fee on Friday, the Holy Day.

ZRANDA. Pushtu term for watermill. See also ASYAB.

BIBLIOGRAPHY

Abercrombie, Thomas J. "Afghanistan: Crossroad of Conquerors," National Geographic Magazine, September, 1968, pp. 297-345.

Adamec, Ludwig W. Afghanistan 1900-1923: A Diplomatic History. Berkeley: University of California Press, 1967.

_____. Afghanistan's Foreign Affairs to the Mid-Twentieth Century. Tucson: University of Arizona Press, 1974.

Akhramovich, R. Concerning the Recent Stages in Afghanistan's Social History. Moscow, 1967.

_____. Outline History of Afghanistan After the Second World War. Moscow, 1967.

Ali, Mohammed. Afghanistan: The National Awakening. Lahore: Educational Press, 1958.

_____. Afghanistan: The Mohammedzai Period. Lahore: Educational Press, 1959.

Amos, Harold. The Story of Afghanistan. Wichita, Kansas: McCormick-Mathers Publishing Company, 1965.

_____. "Dari-Zul: Village in Transition." In: American Historical Anthropology: Essays in Honor of Leslie Spier, C. L. Riley and W. W. Taylor (eds.). Carbondale: Southern Illinois University Press, 1967.

Arberry, A. J. Introduction to the History of Sufism. London, 1942.

_____. Sufism. London: Allen and Unwin, 1950.

Archer, W. "The Music of Afghanistan and Iran," The Society for Asian Music, Quarterly Letter, 1-9, New York, 1964.

Auboyer, Jeanine. The Art of Afghanistan. Middlesex: Hamlyn House, 1968.

Bacon, Elizabeth E. "An Inquiry into the History of the Hazara Mongols of Afghanistan," Southwestern Journal of Anthropology, Vol. 7, 1951, pp. 230-247.

_____. Obok: A Study of Social Structure in Eurasia. New York: Viking Fund Publications in Anthropology, No. 25, Wenner-Gren Publications in Anthropological Research, 1958.

_____. Central Asians Under Russian Rule. Ithaca: Cornell University Press, 1966.

Barret, Parker and Ahmad Javid. A Collection of Afghan Legends. Kabul: Franklin Book Programs, 1970.

Barth, Fredrik. Political Leadership Among Swat Pathans. London School of Economics Monographs in Social Anthropology, No. 19. New York: Humanities Press, 1965.

_____. "Pathan Identity and Its Maintenance." In: Fredrik Barth, Ethnic Groups and Boundaries. Boston: Little, Brown and Company, 1969.

Bell, Marjorie Jewett (ed.). An American Engineer in Afghanistan: From the Letters and Notes of A. C. Jewett. Minneapolis: University of Minnesota Press, 1948.

Bibliography

Bellew, Henry Walter. An Inquiry into the Ethnography of Afghanistan. Woking, England: Oriental Institute, 1891.

Beveridge, A. S. The Babur Nama in English. 2 vols. Translated from the original Turki. London: Luzac, 1922.

Biddulph, C. E. Afghan Poetry of the Seventeenth Century; Being Selections From the Poems of Khush Hal Khan Khatak. London: K. Paul, Trench, Trubner, 1890.

Bosworth, Clifford Edmund. The Ghaznavids: Their Empire in Afghanistan and Eastern Iran, 994-1040. Edinburgh: Edinburgh University Press, 1963.

Boulnois, L. The Silk Route. London, 1966.

Brockelman, Carl. History of the Islamic Peoples. London: Routledge and Kegan Paul, 1949.

Buck, A. A. et al. Health and Disease in Rural Afghanistan. Baltimore: Johns Hopkins University Press, 1972.

Burnes, Alexander. Cabool: A Personal Narrative of a Journey to, and Residence in That City in the Years 1836-38. London: John Murray, 1842.

Cammann, S. "Ancient Symbols in Modern Afghanistan," Ars Orientalis, Vol. 11, 1957, pp. 5-34.

Canfield, Robert L. Faction and Conversion in a Plural Society: Religious Alignment in the Hindu Kush. Anthropological Papers of the Museum of Anthropology 50. Ann Arbor: The University of Michigan, 1973.

_____. "The Ecology of Rural Ethnic Groups and the Spatial Dimension of Power," American Anthropologist, Vol. 75, No. 5, 1973, pp. 1511-1528.

Caroe, Sir Olaf. The Pathans. London: Macmillan, 1958.

Centlivers, Micheline and Pierre and Mark Slobin. "A Muslim Shaman of Afghan Turkestan," Ethnology, Vol. X, No. 2, 1971, pp. 160-173.

Cervin, Vladimir. "Problems in the Integration of the Afghan Nation," Middle East Journal, Vol. 6, 1952, pp. 400-416.

Charpentier, C. J. (ed.). Bazaar-e Tashqurghan: Ethnographical Studies in an Afghan Traditional Bazaar. Uppsala, 1972.

Coon, Carlton. The Seven Caves. New York, 1957.

_____. Caravan: The Story of the Middle East. New York: Holt, Rinehart and Winston, 1958.

Coulson, N. J. A History of Islamic Law. Edinburgh: Edinburgh University Press, 1964.

Cruit, Bette J. Land of the Afghans: A Book for Children. New York: International Publications Service, 1968.

Dames, M. Longworth. The Baloch Race: A Historical and Ethnological Sketch. Asiatic Society Monographs, No. 4. London: Royal Asiatic Society, 1904.

Davis, R. "Prehistoric Investigation in Northern Afghanistan 1969," Afghanistan, Vol. 22, 1970, pp. 75-90.

Debets, G. F. Physical Anthropology of Afghanistan. Cambridge: Peabody Museum, Harvard University, 1970.

Dorn, Bernhard. History of the Afghans. London: Oriental Translation Committee, 1829.

Dupree, Louis. Shamshir Ghar: Historic Cave Site in Kandahar Province, Afghanistan. New York: Anthropological Papers of the American Museum of Natural History, Vol. 46, Pt. 2, 1958.

_____. Deh Morasai Ghundai: A Chalcolithic Site in South-Central Afghanistan. New York: Anthropological Papers of the American Museum of Natural History, Vol. 50, Pt. 2, 1963.

_____. "Aq Kupruk: A Town in North Afghanistan." In: City and Nation in the Developing World, by Associates of the American University Field Staff. New York: American Universities Field Staff, 1966, pp. 5-60.

_____. Afghanistan. Princeton: Princeton University Press, 1974.

_____, et al. Prehistoric Research in Afghanistan (1959-1966). Philadelphia: American Philosophical Society, 1972.

Dupree, Nancy. The Road to Balkh. Kabul: Afghan Tourist Organization, 1967.

_____. The Valley of Bamiyan. Kabul: Afghan Tourist Organization, 1967.

_____. An Historical Guide to Afghanistan. Kabul: Afghan Tourist Organization, 1971.

Dvoryankov, N. A. "The Development of Pushtu as the National and Literary Language of Afghanistan," Central Asian Review, Vol. 24, No. 3, 1966, pp. 210-220.

Eberhard, Wolfram. "Afghanistan's Young Elite." In: Settlement and Social Change in Asia, by Wolfram Eberhard. Hong Kong: Hong Kong University Press, 1967, pp. 397-414.

Elphinstone, Mountstuart. An Account of the Kingdom

of Caubul. London: John Murray, 1857.

Ferdinand, Klaus. Preliminary Notes on the Hazara Culture. Copenhagan, 1959.

_____. "Nomadic Expansion and Commerce in Central Afghanistan: A Sketch of Some Modern Trends," Folk, Vol. 4, 1962, pp. 123-159.

Ferrier, J. P. Caravan Journeys and Wanderings in Persia, Afghanistan, Turkistan and Baloochistan. London: John Murray, 1857.

Field, Neil. "The Amu Darya: A Study in Resource Geography," Geographic Review, XLIV, No. 4, pp. 528-542.

Fletcher, Arnold C. Afghanistan: Highway of Conquest. Ithaca: Cornell University Press, 1965.

Franck, Dorothea S. "Pakhtunistan: Disputed Disposition of a Tribal Land," Middle East Journal, Vol. 6, 1952, pp. 49-68.

Franck, Peter. Afghanistan Between East and West. Washington: National Planning Association, 1960.

Fraser-Tytler, Sir W. Kerr. Afghanistan: A Study of Political Developments in Central and Southern Asia. New York: Paragon Books, 1967.

Freeman-Grenville, G. The Muslim and Christian Calendars. Oxford, 1963.

Gaudefroy-Demombynes, Maurice. Muslim Institutions. London: Allen and Unwin, 1950.

Ghose, Dilip K. England and Afghanistan: A Phase in Their Relations. Calcutta: World Press Private Limited, 1960.

Ghubar, M. Ghulam Mohammed. "The Role of Afghanistan in the Civilization of Islam," Afghanistan,

Vol. I, No. 1, 1946, pp. 26-33.

_____. The Course of Afghanistan in History. Kabul: Government Printing Office, 1967. (In Dari. The title in Dari reads, Afghanistan Dar Maseer-i-Tarikh.)

Gibb, H. A. R. The Arab Conquests in Central Asia. London: Royal Asiatic Society, 1923.

Gibb, H. A. R. and J. H. Kramer. Shorter Encyclopedia of Islam. Ithaca: Cornell University Press, 1957.

Gillet, Michael. "Afghanistan," Royal Central Asian Journal, Vol. LIII, Pt. 3, October 1966, pp. 238-244.

Grassmuck, George, et al. (eds.). Afghanistan: Some New Approaches. Ann Arbor: The University of Michigan Press, 1969.

Gregorian, Vartan. The Emergence of Modern Afghanistan. Stanford: Stanford University Press, 1969.

Griffiths, John C. Afghanistan. New York: Praeger, 1967.

Grunebaum, Gustav von. Mohammadan Festivals. New York, 1951.

Habberton, William. Anglo-Russian Relations Concerning Afghanistan, 1837-1907. Urbana: University of Illinois Press, 1937.

Habib, Abd-al Haqq. A Short History of Calligraphy and Epigraphy in Afghanistan. Kabul: The Historical and Literary Society of Afghanistan Academy, 1971.

Habibullah, Amir. My Life: From Brigand to King. London: Sampson Low, Marston, n. d.

Hambly, Gavin. *Central Asia*. New York: Delacorte Press, 1969.

Hamilton, Angus. *Afghanistan*. London: William Heinemann, 1906.

Hanifi, M. Jamil. "Child Rearing Patterns Among Pushtuns of Afghanistan," *International Journal of the Sociology of the Family*, Vol. 1, No. 1, 1971, pp. 53-57.

_____. "Cultural Diversity, Conflicting Ideologies, and Transformational Processes in Afghanistan." In: *Asian-African Hot and Cold Desert and Steppe*, edited by Wolfgang Weissleder. Proceedings of the IXth International Congress of Anthropological and Ethnological Sciences. The Hague: Mouton, 1974.

_____. *Islam and the Transformation of Culture*. New York: The Asia Publishing House, 1974.

_____. "Pre-Industrial Kabul: Its Structure and Function in Transformational Processes in Afghanistan." In: *Mutual Interaction of People and Their Built Environment*, edited by Amos Rapaport. Proceedings of the IXth International Congress of Anthropological and Ethnological Sciences. The Hague: Mouton, 1974.

_____. *The Central Asian City and Its Role in Cultural Transformation*. New York: Afghanistan Council, The Asia Society (occasional paper No. 6), 1974.

Huffman, Arthur V. "The Administrative and Social Structure of Afghan Life," *Journal of the Royal Central Asian Society*, Vol. 38, 1951, pp. 41-48.

Iqbal, Mohammed. "Kushhal Khan Khatak: The Afghan Warrior-Poet," *Islamic Culture*, Vol. 2, 1928, pp. 485-494.

Jarring, Gunnar. Uzbek Texts From Afghan Turkistan. Lunds Universitets Arsskrift, N. F. Avd. 1, Bd. 34, Nr. 2. Lund: C. W. K. Gleerup, 1938.

──────. On the Distribution of Turk Tribes in Afghanistan: An Attempt at a Preliminary Classification. Lund: Lunds Universitets Arsskrift, N. F., Ard. 1, Bd. 35, Nr. 4, C. W. K. Gleerup, 1939.

Jones, Schuyler. The Political Organization of the Kam Kafirs. Copenhagen, 1967.

──────. An Annotated Bibliography of Nuristan (Kafiristan) and the Kalash Kafirs of Chitral. Copenhagen, Part I, 1966; Part II, 1969.

Kakar, M. Hasan. Afghanistan: A Study in Internal Political Development 1880-1896. Lahore, Pakistan: Punjab Educational Press, 1971.

──────. The Pacification of the Hazaras of Afghanistan. New York: Afghanistan Council, The Asia Society (occasional paper series No. 4), 1973.

Kamrany, Nake M. Peaceful Competition in Afghanistan. Washington: Communication Service Corporation, 1969.

Keiser, Lincoln. Genealogical Beliefs and Social Structure Among the Sum of Afghanistan: A Study of Custom in the Context of Social Relations. New York: Afghanistan Council, The Asian Society (occasional paper No. 5), 1973.

Kennedy, T. F. Afghanistan Village. Netley, South Australia: The Griffin Press, 1967.

Kessel, Joseph. The Horsemen. New York: Farrar, Straus and Giroux, 1968.

Klass, Rossane. Land of the High Flags. New York: Random House, 1964.

Kohzad, Ahmad Ali. Men and Events Through Eighteenth
and Nineteenth Century Afghanistan. New York:
International Publications Service, 1969.

Konishi, Mosatoshi. Afghanistan: Crossroads of the
Ages. Tokyo: Kondosha International, 1969.

Lal, Mohan. Life of the Ameer Dost Mohammed Khan
of Kabul. 2 Vols. London: Longman, Brown,
Green and Longman, 1846.

Lumsden, Peter. "Countries and Tribes Bordering on
the Koh-i-Baba Range," Royal Geographical Society, Vol. 7, 1885, pp. 561-583.

McKeller, Doris. Afghan Cooking. New York: International Publications Service, 1967.

MacMunn, George F. Afghanistan From Darius to
Amanullah. London: G. Bell and Sons, 1929.

Maranjian, G. "The Distribution of ABO Blood Groups
in Afghanistan," American Journal of Physical
Anthropology, Vol. 10, 1958, p. 263.

Mattai, James. A Geographical Introduction to Herat
Province. Kabul: Kabul University Press, 1966.

Mayne, Peter. Journey to the Pathans. New York:
Doubleday, 1955.

Michaud, Sabrina and Roland. "Turkomans, Horsemen
of the Steppes," National Geographic Magazine,
November 1973, pp. 634-669.

Michel, Aloys A. The Kabul, Kunduz, and Helmand
Valleys and the National Economy of Afghanistan.
Washington: National Academy of Sciences, 1959.

Michener, James. Caravans. New York: Random
House, 1963.

Mir Munshi, Sultan Mohammed Khan (ed.). The Life

of Abdur Rahman, Amir of Afghanistan. 2 Vols.
London: John Murray, 1900.

Mirepoix, Camille. Afghanistan in Pictures. New
York: Sterling Publishing Company, 1971.

Morgenstierne, Georg. Report on a Linguistic Mission
to Afghanistan. Instituttet for Sammenlignende
Kulturforskning, 1-2 series C. Oslo: H. Aschehoug, 1926.

_____. Report on a Linguistic Mission to North-
western India. Instituttet for Sammenlignende
Kulturforskning, 3-1 series C. Oslo: H.
Aschehoug, 1932.

_____. Indo-Iranian Frontier Languages. Volume 1
(Parachi and Ormuri); Volume 2 (Iranian Pamir
Languages); Volume 3 (The Pashai Language).
Instituttet for Sammenlignende Kulturforskning,
series B. Oslo: H. Aschehoug, Vol. 1, 1929;
Vol. 2, 1938; Vol. 3, 1944.

Nazim, Muhammed. The Life and Times of Sultan
Mahmud of Ghazna. Cambridge: Cambridge
University Press, 1931.

Newell, Richard S. The Politics of Afghanistan.
Ithaca: Cornell University Press, 1972.

Oliver, Edward M. Across the Border: Pathan and
Baloch. London: Chapman and Hall, 1890.

Paludan, K. On the Birds of Afghanistan. Copenhagen,
1959.

Pandey, Awadh. The First Afghan Empire in India,
1451-1526. Calcutta: Bookland, 1956.

Patai, Raphael. "The Middle East as a Culture Area,"
Middle East Journal, Vol. 6, 1952, pp. 1-22.

Pazhwak, Abdur Rahman. Aryana (Ancient Afghanistan).

Hove, England: Key Press, 1954.

_____. Pakhtunsitan: The Khyber Pass as the Focus of the New State of Pakhtunistan. Hove, England: Key Press, 1954.

Pehrson, Robert (Compiled from his notes by Fredrik Barth). The Social Organization of the Marri Baluch. Chicago: Aldine Publishing Company, 1966.

Penzil, Herbert. A Grammar of Pashto: A Descriptive Study of the Dialect of Kandahar, Afghanistan. Washington: American Council of Learned Societies, 1955.

Poullada, Leon B. Reform and Rebellion in Afghanistan 1919-1929: King Amanulla's Failure to Modernize a Tribal Society. Ithaca: Cornell University Press, 1973.

Ramazani, Rouhollah K. Northern Tier: Southern Borderlands of the Soviet Union. New York: Van Nostrand, 1966.

Recent Books About Afghanistan: A Selected, Annotated Bibliography 1968-1973. New York: Afghanistan Council, The Asia Society, 1973.

Rice, Francis M. and Benjamine Rowland. Art in Afghanistan. Objects From the Kabul Museum. Coral Gables: University of Miami Press, 1971.

Robertson, George Scott. The Kafirs of the Hindu-Kush. London: Lawrence and Bullen, 1896. (Reprinted in 1970.)

Rowland, B. Ancient Art in Afghanistan. New York: The Asia Society, 1966.

Sale, Lady Florentia. A Journal of Disasters in Afghanistan, 1841-2. London: John Murray, 1843.

Schurmann, H. F. The Mongols of Afghanistan: An Ethnography of the Mongols and Related Peoples of Afghanistan. The Hague: Mouton, 1962.

Scott, George B. Afghan and Pathan: A Sketch. London: Mitre Press, 1929.

Shah, Idies. The Exploits of the Incomparable Mulla Nasrudin. 1967.

Shor, Jean Bowie. After You, Marco Polo. New York: McGraw-Hill, 1955.

Siiger, H. "Shamanism Among the Kalash Kafirs of Chitral," Folk, Vol. 5, 1963, pp. 295-305.

Singh, Ganda. Ahmad Shah Durrani: Father of Modern Afghanistan. Bombay: Asia Publishing House, 1959.

Spain, James W. People of the Khyber. New York: Praeger, 1963.

_____. The Pathan Borderland. The Hague: Mouton, 1963.

Stewart, Rhea T. Fire in Afghanistan. New York: Doubleday, 1973.

Survey of Progress 1969-1970. Afghanistan, Ministry of Planning. Kabul: Ministry of Planning, 1970.

Sykes, Percy M. A History of Afghanistan. 2 Vols. London: Macmillan, 1940.

Tarn, W. The Greeks in Bactria and India. Cambridge: Cambridge University Press, 1951.

Tate, George Passman. The Frontier of Baluchistan: Travels on the Borders of Persia and Afghanistan. London: Witherby, 1909.

_____. The Kingdom of Afghanistan: A Historical

Sketch. Bombay: Times of India Offices, 1911.

Tilman, H. W. "Wakhan: Or How to Vary a Route," Journal of the Royal Central Asian Society, Vol. 35, 1948, pp. 249-254.

Trinkler, Emil. Through the Heart of Afghanistan. Edited and translated by B. K. Featherstone. Boston: Houghton-Mifflin, 1928.

Trousdale, W. "The Minaret of Jam: A Ghorid Monument in Afghanistan," Archaeology, Vol. 18, No. 2, 1965, pp. 102-108.

Ullah, Najib. Islamic Literature: An Introductory History with Selections. New York: Washington Square Press, 1963.

Varma, Birendra. English East India Company and the Afghans, 1757-1800. Calcutta: Punthi Pustak, 1968.

Warburton, Robert. Eighteen Years in the Khyber 1879-1898. London: John Murray, 1900.

Watkins, Mary B. Afghanistan: Land in Transition. New York: D. Van Nostrand Company, Inc., 1963.

Weston, Christine. Afghanistan. New York: Charles Scribner's Sons, 1962.

Wilbur, Donald N. "The Structure of Islam in Afghanistan," Middle East Journal, Vol. 6, No. 1, 1952, pp. 41-48.

_____. Afghanistan: Its People, Its Society, Its Culture. New Haven: Human Relations Area Files, 1962.

_____. An Annotated Bibliography of Afghanistan. New Haven: Human Relations Area Files, 1968.

Wilson, Andrew. "Inside Afghanistan: A Background to Recent Events," Royal Central Asian Journal, Vol. 47, 1960, pp. 286-295.

_____. North From Kabul. London: George Allen and Unwin Ltd., 1961.

Wilson, J. Christie, Jr. An Introduction to Colloquial Kabul Persian. Presidio of Monterey, California: Army Language School, 1955.

Wolfe, Nancy (Nancy Dupree). Herat, A Pictorial Guide. Kabul: Afghan Tourist Organization, 1966.

_____. In Collaboration with Ahmad Ali Kohzad. An Historical Guide to Kabul. Kabul: Afghan Tourist Organization, 1965.

Wood-Walker, R. et al. "The Blood Groups of the Timuri and Related Tribes in Afghanistan," American Journal of Physical Anthropology, Vol. 27, No. 2, 1967, pp. 195-204.

Wulff, Hans E. The Traditional Crafts of Persia. Cambridge: The M.I.T. Press, 1966.

Yate, Charles Edward. "Notes on the City of Herat," Journal of the Asiatic Society of Bengal, Vol. 56, pp. 84-106.

_____. Northern Afghanistan: Letters for the Afghan Boundary Commission. London: W. Blackwood, 1888.

Zaehner, R. The Dawn and Twilight of Zoroastrianism. London, 1961.

Zeigler, J. "Geological Study of Shamshir Ghar Cave, Southern Afghanistan, and Report of Terraces Along Panjshir Valley Near Kabul," Journal of Geology, Vol. 66, No. 1, 1958, pp. 16-27.